HEROES OF PEACE

HEROES OF PEACE

BY

ARCHER WALLACE

Author of

"BLAZING NEW TRAILS," "STORIES OF GRIT,"
"OVERCOMING HANDICAPS," AND "CANADIAN
HEROES OF MISSION FIELDS OVERSEAS"

136957

TORONTO
THE MUSSON BOOK COMPANY
LIMITED

16

PRINTED IN CANADA
T. H. BEST PRINTING CO., LIMITED
TORONTO, ONT.

CONTENTS

BEFORE YOU BEGIN

FRIEND READER:

You will be interested in a word about Archer Wallace, whose stories of peace-time adventure and heroism you are about to enjoy. Well, he's a Canadian, although, through the wide circulation of his books, he is almost as well known in the United States and Great Britain as in Canada.

If you were a boy in Toronto, particularly one who plays hockey well enough to have a place on one of the crack amateur teams of that part of the world, you would hardly escape knowing this genial, enthusiastic man who has followed this "fastest sport of them all" for years because he loves the game and, even more, the boys who play it.

All his life a lover of boys, he has spent some ten years as a worker among them; indeed he has never quite outgrown being a boy himself. He is now the editor of as attractive a little weekly magazine as ever whetted a boy's appetite for more. He knows the kind of story a real boy likes, and he knows how to tell it to suit a boy's taste.

So whether you are as old as Archer Wallace or as young as the heart of him, you are right now just the turn of a page or two away from my idea of a wonderful time. The doorway to new adventures stands ajar inviting you in. Step into the cockpit with "Lindy" and ride the sky with the Lone Eagle as he conquers the broad Atlantic. Stand with fearless William Penn under a great elm on the Susquehanna and see the grateful surprise on the Indians' faces as he says: "We come to meet you without guns or swords, with only good will and love in our hearts." Travel with Albert Schweitzer into the heart of Africa and thrill to hear the awestruck natives explain how their beloved surgeon "kills the sick people, then cures them, and after that he wakes them up again." Watch George Washington Carver in his laboratory change sweet potatoes into rubber and candy and shoe polish and breakfast food, using the money he makes to educate his fellow Negroes. Follow George Williams and a group of earnest young business men up into a bedroom in a London lodging house and listen in on the beginnings of what is now the world-wide Y. M. C. A.

There are fifteen of the stories, and long before you have come to the last of them you'll have added new heroes to your own personal hall of fame. You will find your ideas about heroes changing too, as you discover here how it is that the world grows better, not by the doings of warlike kings and conquerors, but because great doctors and explorers and missionaries and inventors and engineers have put glory and romance and a spirit of unselfish service into their labours.

If you were to call on Archer Wallace and quizz him, as I have, about what started him writing his books for boys, he would undoubtedly answer you, as he has me, "I know there is a time in every boy's life when he needs encouragement; a push in the right direction then will be a blessing to him and, who knows, perhaps a great big boost for the world into the bargain."

You'll not wonder therefore when you find written between the lines of these adventures in service a kind of irresistible encouragement which grips a boy and says: "Young fellow, my lad, 'Go thou and do likewise!'"

Yes, and he'll make you believe you can, too.

ALFRED D. MOORE

Editor in Charge of Story Papers for the Church Schools of the Methodist Episcopal Church, Cincinnati, Ohio.

COLONEL CHARLES A. LINDBERGH

"The Lone Eagle"

ON THE morning of May 20, 1927, a number of keenly interested people gathered at Roosevelt Field, on the outskirts of New York City, to witness the start of a very daring adventure. Charles A. Lindbergh, a young man twenty-five years of age, had announced his intention of flying alone from New York to Paris, a feat which no one had previously accomplished and which few, if any, thought young Lindbergh could do. Just a few days previously two brave Frenchmen, Nungesser and Coli, had attempted to fly from Paris to New York. The attempt had a tragic end as nothing more was ever heard of the two aviators; doubtless they perished in the cold waters of the Atlantic.

While admiring his courage, many of Lindbergh's best friends and admirers shook their heads when he set out on his daring adventure; others, more critical, ridiculed the whole thing and said it was a foolhardy adventure which was bound to end in failure.

Charles Lindbergh, who was born in Detroit on February 4, 1902, saw his first airplane when he was ten years of age, and was fascinated by it. There and then he resolved that some day he would be an aviator. After graduating from high school he decided to study mechanical engineering and became a student at Wisconsin University. While there he became more than ever interested in aëronautics, and when as a passenger he took his first flight on April 9, 1922, it gave him a great thrill. He enrolled as a student with the Nebraska Aircraft Corporation and at once began to receive instruction in flying. He was a willing and eager pupil and it was not long before he was doing "solo" flying, as flying alone is termed.

His father had never been in an airplane and was opposed to Charles flying, but one day the young flier persuaded his father to take a trip. Rather dubiously Mr. Lindbergh climbed into the cockpit of the machine and in a few minutes he was enjoying his first ride. From that day he never said a word against Charles flying and never missed an opportunity of having a ride in the plane. Unlike her husband, Mrs. Lindbergh had been in sympathy with her son's ambition from the beginning. She went up in his machine the first chance she got and became almost as enthusiastic as he was.

Soon after this Lindbergh entered the training school for cadets in the Air Service of the United States Government. He underwent many very exacting tests and at the end of a year was granted a commission as second lieutenant in the Air Service Reserve Corps. Out of one hundred and four cadets who began the course only eighteen were successful.

It was in the fall of 1926 that Charles Lindbergh first thought of the New York to Paris trip. He knew that it would not be easy but the more he thought about it the more convinced he became that he could make it. When he first mentioned the matter some scoffed at and others opposed his venture but fortunately there were some public-spirited men in St. Louis, where he lived, to support the project and give him encouragement. He began to lay his plans carefully. He thought of every possible difficulty that might arise and left nothing to chance. When the plane, which he named *The Spirit of St. Louis,* rested at Curtiss Field on the morning of May 20, 1927, there was nothing about it that Lindbergh did not know and had not studied carefully.

It was just twenty minutes to eight when

Charles Lindbergh, with millions of people on both sides of the Atlantic thinking of him, slowly rose from the soft mud of the field and set out on one of the most thrilling adventures in all history. The plane did not rise rapidly but mounted high enough for him to glide over some tall trees on a hill and soon he reached Long Island Sound, where the Curtiss Oriole machine, with a photographer on board, turned back and Lindbergh faced the journey of three thousand six hundred miles alone.

There was considerable haze for a time but this cleared and he made the three hundred miles from Cape Cod to Nova Scotia in good time. As he flew north he saw here and there patches of snow and to the eastward there was fog. He passed over St. John's, Newfoundland, and as evening drew on he could see the white icebergs shining with surprising clearness through the darkness.

There was no moon at first and it was very dark. Clouds were dense and it was risky to try to penetrate through them. Once, when he attempted to fly through a large cloud, sleet began to gather on his plane and he was forced to turn back and get into clear air immediately. After that he flew around clouds which he could not climb over. After a few hours of darkness the moon appeared and this greatly helped him.

He flew steadily on through the night with no sound but that of his throbbing engine. When the first gray streaks of dawn came, he saw broken clouds ahead, some of which he surmounted, in other cases he flew through them. Then holes began to appear in the fog and through one of them he saw the sea. He dropped down until he was within one hundred feet of the water and he could see the whitecaps dancing upon the waves. A blinding fog made it necessary for him to mount up again as high as fifteen hundred feet but when it cleared he dropped down to near the water again; sometimes as close as ten feet.

He saw several porpoises in the water but for several hours no ships. His first intimation that he was approaching the European side of the Atlantic was the sight of a small fishing vessel; soon he saw others, and on one of them he saw a man's astonished face appear at the cabin window. He flew as near to the little ships as he dared and shouted: "Which way is Ireland?" Evidently the men did not hear him as he got no answer.

Less than an hour afterwards a rugged and mountainous coastline appeared to the northeast. The shore, which was ten or fifteen miles away, was fairly distinct. A light haze, coupled with local storm areas, had prevented him seeing the land sooner, which, of course, was Ireland.

After passing over Ireland he saw several steamers and in about two hours' time he sighted the coast of England. Then he began the last lap of his journey toward France. Before long he sighted Cherbourg and very soon afterward he saw the lights of Paris. This was about five P. M. New York time and ten P. M. Paris time. He circled the famous Eiffel Tower at an altitude of four thousand feet and then flew toward Le Bourget, where he intended to land. He flew around the field once, then landed. His wonderful adventure was over, his great feat successfully accomplished. He had been in the air thirty-three hours and thirty minutes, had flown three thousand six hundred miles, and established a new and remarkable record.

The entire field where he landed was covered with thousands of people who swarmed around his plane like so many bees. He was concerned about his beloved plane and tried to get the crowd to keep back, but either they did not understand him or were determined to give him a glorious welcome at any cost. He started to get out of the cockpit of his machine and was dragged the rest of the way, then was carried round and round the field for half an hour.

Lindbergh received a tremendously enthusiastic reception in France and this was but a foretaste of what was to follow in Belgium, Great Britain, and in his own country, the United States. Although but a youth he was the first airman to fly across the Atlantic alone and the attention of millions was directed toward him. Probably no man in all history received as much flattering attention as did Charles Lindbergh.

As soon as he could free himself from the mobs, he had a telephone conversation with his mother in Detroit, four thousand miles away. Then he called on Madame Nungesser, whose equally brave son had disappeared only a few days previously, in the Atlantic waters he had crossed. He completely won the hearts of the French people by frankly telling them that Nungesser and Coli had attempted a much more difficult feat than his, when they attempted to fly from Paris to New York. His modesty and charmingly frank disposition won for him a place in the hearts of the French people from the beginning. It would be impossible to mention here all the honours which came to Lindbergh during the next few months. The President of the French Republic pinned the Cross of the Legion of Honour upon his coat. It appeared as if every great organization in France wanted to do him honour, and no one seemed more surprised than Lindbergh, who was deeply touched and often quite embarrassed by so much praise. He lunched with Bleriot, the first man to fly across the English Channel, who presented him with a piece of his plane. He had a notable visit from the great military leader, Marshal Foch. He visited the hospitals where invalided soldiers of the Great War gave him a great welcome, and then called upon Marshal Joffre in his home.

In Brussels he was cordially received at the royal palace by King Albert of Belgium. The King and Queen were both greatly interested in examining *The Spirit of St. Louis* and Lindbergh explained its technical features. The welcome of the Belgian people everywhere was enthusiastic and affectionate.

When Lindbergh landed at Croydon Field on the outskirts of London, it is estimated that he was welcomed by a crowd of half a million people. As in France and Belgium Lindbergh was received with unbounded enthusiasm and he received ample evidence of the good sportsmanship of the English people. In Westminster Abbey he laid a wreath on the tomb of the Unknown Soldier on which was inscribed: "In memory of England's unknown warrior, from the American people." On May 31st, he was received by King George V, who set aside all precedent and personally presented him with the Royal Air Force

Cross. Later Lindbergh was warmly received and congratulated by the Prince of Wales and by the Hon. Stanley Baldwin, Prime Minister of Great Britain.

It would be impossible to write fully here of the welcome Lindbergh received in the United States. Indeed, from the standpoint of numbers and from the enthusiasm shown, he received the greatest welcome accorded to any man in history. In Washington, where President and Mrs. Coolidge officially greeted him, later in New York, then in Chicago and other cities, and in St. Louis, his home—it was the same everywhere; the enthusiasm of the people knew no bounds. In St. Louis ten thousand school children signed a petition asking him to visit his home city with *The Spirit of St. Louis*. People went wild over him. One New York newspaper alone received fifteen hundred poems about his wonderful adventure.

Throughout these weeks and months of flattering receptions Charles Lindbergh remained the same modest, unassuming and open-hearted American youth. Those who were close to him during these days declare that the way he kept his head and remained unspoiled and free from vanity was an achievement as great, if not even greater, than crossing the Atlantic alone. Not one in ten thousand could have done it, but it was a lesson in modesty that the world will never forget. Hundreds of money-making propositions were made to Lindbergh; great moving-picture concerns wanted him to be filmed and pose as a hero. All of them he courteously but firmly turned down. "Gentlemen," he said, "I am not for sale."

When people are asked what they consider to be the greatest thing that Lindbergh ever did, many will think of that moment when, in the gray dawn of a May morning, the brave young flier set out for Paris. But others will think of him as he was when great honours were heaped upon him day after day; when kings were honoured to receive him and great men proud to shake his hand. And they will remember how modest, how unspoiled and gracious he remained throughout it all. "This," they will say, "was the greatest thing Charles Lindbergh ever did."

II

SIR ERNEST SHACKLETON

Who Loved to Do Hard Things

IN OCTOBER, 1915, the ship *Endurance*, under command of the explorer Sir Ernest Shackleton, was held fast in the terrible grip of the Antarctic ice. In December, 1914, the *Endurance* had left South Georgia; the intervening ten months had been spent by the twenty-eight members of the crew amid the dreary wastes of ice in polar seas. During the previous winter they had not seen the sun for seventy-nine days in succession. Many of the dogs, upon which they relied so much in travelling, had died through disease and the food supply was steadily diminishing.

Sir Ernest Shackleton struggled hard to keep the *Endurance* free in the open ice and to prevent it from being jammed by the gigantic boulders, but on October 24th she was caught between three huge masses. One pressed against the starboard side, a second against the port quarter twisting the ship and causing her to leak seriously. A third ice floe crashed into the bow; seemed to climb over the forecastle and force the gallant little ship down by the head.

Every man worked hard at the pumps but from the beginning it was useless. The planks in the ship began to strain and crack. The rudder post was smashed by one terrific blow, the decks broke up, and water rushed in. Shackleton and every man on board knew that the *Endurance* would never float again and so at four o'clock on October 27th Sir Ernest and the twenty-seven members of his crew left her, taking whatever was likely to be of use to them in the terrible predicament in which they found themselves. The little ship had ploughed her way through one thousand five hundred miles of ice, but now she was a prisoner and soon after the crew left her sides were smashed in as though she were made of eggshell.

Hastily tents were set up on the large masses of ice. Baffled and disappointed, Sir Ernest Shackleton paced alone in the darkness, turning over in his mind first one plan then another whereby he might get his comrades over the thousand miles of sea and ice which separated them from the nearest dwelling places of men. The crew were not panic-stricken by any means but the amazing courage and cheerfulness of Shackleton had a tremendous influence over them. No matter how

weary and worried he might be within, outwardly
he was calm, cheerful, and confident. Never once
did a word of discouragement cross his lips, and
when the men looked at him they too smiled con-
fidently.

Sir Ernest stood with his men upon a cracked
and crumpled ice floe drifting vaguely on and on,
knowing that any minute the floe might break and
plung them into the icy sea. After many weary
weeks of life upon the ice a dash was made for
Elephant Island and here the party landed on
April 15, 1916, after a terrible experience. Shackleton, upon whose shoulders rested the whole respon-
sibility for the venture, was so exhausted that after
eight sleepless nights he lay down upon the beach
and slept untroubled by the damp and cold.

The party had with them three small boats and
after three days of hard thinking Shackleton decided to take the *James Caird,* the largest of the
three, and, leaving most of the crew behind, attempt to reach a whaling station in South Georgia,
eight hundred miles away. It seemed almost like a
mad adventure, yet it was the only thing to do
as there was no hope of rescue at Elephant Island.
The *James Caird* was only twenty-two feet long
and seven feet at her widest, yet in this little craft
Shackleton and five other men left Elephant
Island on the morning of April 24th.

The little boat slipped through a lane of ice into the open sea on her perilous voyage and as she set out the twenty-two men who were left behind gave a rousing cheer. All their hopes of being saved from a horrible death rested with that small boat and the six brave men she carried.

Shackleton and the five men with him were already nearly exhausted by the terrible experiences of the winter through which they had come. Their clothing was torn and tattered; their skin flayed at every joint with horrible sea blisters caused by salt water, cold, and rough clothing. They dared not stand up except for a moment or so at a time, and they were unable to lie down. Often they were so cramped that they could not bend their knees. Had it not been for the amazing courage and cheerfulness of Shackleton the voyage must have ended in disaster, but he was always seeking some pretext for a joke and through the long weary hours the men kept their spirits up. Sometimes the little craft seemed a mere speck between waves that rose up like mountains. More than once it seemed as if the end had come and the *James Caird* would be smothered but, like some charmed cork, she bobbed up again. Several times great albatrosses, almost as big as the boat itself, followed them, no doubt expecting to devour the six men who looked so helpless. "Don't worry, boys," shouted Shackleton, "we're going to get through all right." Did ever so small a boat successfully battle through such angry seas? The spray froze upon the sides of the boat until it looked as if it were clothed in a coat of white mail. The men were drenched to the skin, half frozen by the cold, and almost famished for want of food. They were nearly maddened by the shortage of water, and blinded by snowstorms, but they battled their way through it all till land loomed up in the distance.

On the morning of May 8th, the mountains of South Georgia came into view. A terrific storm almost wrecked them when land was in view, but two days later the little boat slipped into a cove with the men absolutely exhausted. Two of the men were quite ill and Shackleton decided to take the other two and attempt to cross the mountains to the whaling station, seventeen miles away. At three o'clock in the morning of May 19th the tramp across the snowclad mountains began. It was the last and perhaps the most difficult lap of that great adventure, for no one had ever scaled these mountains before. The three men took only three days' provisions along with them as it was thought wise to take the least possible luggage.

The first day they climbed 2,500 feet and were often over the ankles in snow. When night came

moonlight revealed to them high peaks, impass-
able cliffs, and sharply descending glaciers. Then
a heavy fog descending made it necessary for them
to rope themselves together lest one should
stumble over a precipice or be plunged into a deep
crevasse. On and on they dragged their weary
limbs across the mountains. Their weariness was
such that at times they seemed scarcely awake.
There was the constant temptation to lie down in
the snow and sleep, but from such a sleep there
would have been no awakening. That which kept
them going on was the thought of the twenty-two
marooned men on Elephant Island and the three
they had just left. They did not speak of this but
no matter what they talked about, the thought of
the suffering men was constantly in their minds
and for their sakes they kept plodding on and
on. It was a strange land to them, they had little
protection against the cold, and there was only a
step between them and death; yet their accom-
plishment was what now looks like a superhuman
task.

The whaling station came into view. Solemnly
the weary men shook hands. "Boss," said one to
Shackleton, "it looks too good to be true." As
they neared the colony they saw some children—
the first human beings except their crew they had
seen since December, 1914. The children fled from

them terror-stricken. But soon they were comfortably housed and the terrible experience was at an end.

It was just like Shackleton not to be able to sleep, weary though he was, until the three men who had been left at the other side of the mountain had been sent for, and then he began to make plans to rescue the twenty-two men on Elephant Island. After many disappointments, at last the Chilean government loaned him the little steel-built ship, *Yelcho*, to make a dash for Elephant Island. The island was reached on August 30th and as they sailed along the coast, eagerly looking for the stranded men, they sighted the camp just about the same time as the men, almost starved and half crazed with fatigue and anxiety, saw them.

A little boat put off from the *Yelcho* with Shackleton standing in the bow. "Are you all well?" roared Shackleton as they neared the shore. "Yes, Boss, we are all well," came the answer. Even from a distance the men could see the smile that lighted up his face when he said: "Thank God." Every day for weeks the marooned men on Elephant Island had said to one another, "Perhaps the Boss will come to-day." When at last the rescuing boat did draw near they instantly recognized Shackleton's figure in the boat and cheered. For four months the men had been left on the island; they had suffered terrible hardships and their provisions were almost exhausted, but the story of their rescue is one of the most thrilling that can ever be told.

Shackleton and his men reached Punta Arenas on September 3d and they were given a great reception by the warm-hearted Chileans. A public holiday was proclaimed and the entire population turned out to welcome and honour the survivors. In the presence of thirty thousand spectators the President of the Republic presented Shackleton with the Chilean Order of Merit.

In New Zealand and then, some months later, in the United States, Shackleton received tremendous ovations. His simple, straightforward, and modest manner of telling the story of his adventures and those of his men aroused enthusiasm wherever he spoke. At San Francisco his address was heard with rapt attention by eight thousand people. By the end of May, 1917, he reached England. He was received by King George V, who, in the name of the nation, greeted him warmly; then he joined his wife and children from whom he had been separated so long.

After a period of rest Sir Ernest Shackleton planned another expedition. To the wide-open spaces of the Southern seas his mind turned again and again. As long as there were unknown regions he felt it to be a call to endeavour. And so on the ship *Quest*, he sailed from Plymouth on September 24, 1921, on what proved to be his last voyage. He was as light hearted as a boy and his cheeriness spread to everybody on board. Rio de Janeiro was reached on November 22d. From there he wrote to a friend: "All the work is done. The next you will hear will be, please God, success. Should anything happen it will not be because of anything wrong with the ship. The ship is all right."

Never for me the lowered banner,
Never the lost endeavour!

Soon after reaching South Georgia Shackleton was taken seriously ill. Years of exposure and severe hardship had undermined his constitution and he died at half-past three on the morning of January 5, 1922.

His splendid life is a constant reminder that the deepest satisfaction comes not from self-indulgence but by the path of heroic self-sacrifice. Brave, kind, unselfish, he found his deepest joy in doing hard things; every difficulty was a challenge to this true hero.

III

ALBERT SCHWEITZER

A HERO IN THE AFRICAN JUNGLE

WHEN Albert Schweitzer, a boy living at Mülhausen in Alsace, was compelled to take piano lessons he did not enjoy them any more than most other boys do. Eugen Munch, his teacher, insisted upon Albert playing exercises, frequently for hours at a time, whereas he longed to play familiar airs and tunes he had composed himself. Therefore it was often a rebellious boy with a tear-stained face who sat down at the piano.

One day the teacher discovered what a genius Albert had for music and promised him that soon he would be permitted to have lessons on the beautiful organ in the church. It was a big organ, with three keyboards and sixty-two stops, and the fifteen-year-old boy could hardly believe his good fortune. But play on it he did and so well that frequently he was allowed to play for the whole church service and on such important occasions as special concerts, so that while still a mere boy,

Albert Schweitzer seemed destined to become a great musician.

Albert's father was a minister and on the first Sunday afternoon in every month there was a missionary service in the church and Albert listened eagerly as his father told of people living in distant lands. He was especially interested in Africa and the millions of black people living there. Not far away at Colmar there lived a great sculptor named Bartholdi. This was the man who made the figure of Liberty which stands at the entrance of New York harbour. Bartholdi had made a great statue which stood in the Champ de Mars at Colmar. It was of a giant Negro with a sad and lonely expression as though some great burden rested upon his weary shoulders. Every time Albert visited Colmar he went to look at that statue and to gaze intently upon every feature of that troubled face. It made him think of the millions of poor people living in the Dark Continent.

Later Albert Schweitzer attended Strassburg University and graduated with high honours. He also cultivated his remarkable musical gifts and frequently gave recitals which excited great enthusiasm. His wonderful ability was recognized by everybody. But he never forgot the missionary sermons he had heard in his father's church, nor could he get out of his mind Bartholdi's statue of the unhappy Negro. He knew that in the African forests there were millions of Negroes living in misery. It was the thought of these people's miseries which caused him to begin the study of medicine when he was nearly thirty years of age, and which led him to abandon an important position in Strassburg University, where he had become a professor of literature, and also to give up a most promising career as a musician in order to go into the dark African jungle and heal the sick.

The church bells in the Alsatian village of Gunsbach had just ceased ringing for the afternoon service on Good Friday, 1913, when the train appeared round the corner of the wood and Albert Schweitzer with his wife got on board and the long journey to Africa began. His destination was the mission station at Lambarene, far up the Ogome River, on the west coast.

After sailing many miles up the Ogome, past virgin forests and many strange tribes, the missionaries arrived one evening at Lambarene. A little band of Negro Christians gave them a warm welcome. Little children had decorated the bungalow which was to be the missionaries' home with palms and flowers, and so, far inland, surrounded by deep jungles and all manner of strange

animals and sorely distressed people, Albert
Schweitzer began his work of healing the sick and
preaching the gospel.

The news that there was a doctor at the mission station spread rapidly. Dr. Schweitzer announced that only serious cases could be treated
during the first three weeks, but not much attention was paid to this. Sick people began to ar-
rive at every hour of the day and night and the
doctor could scarcely find time to unpack his
trunks. Dr. Schweitzer had been presented by
some friends in Paris with a piano especially built
for the tropics and he managed to get this instrument safely into his African bungalow, where it
was a never-failing source of interest and delight
to the astonished natives. Among the patients who
came for treatment was an intelligent native
named Joseph who spoke French remarkably well.
He acted as interpreter for the missionary and
helped as assistant when surgical operations had
to be performed.

A building previously used as a fowl house had
to serve as consulting room and clinic. Consulting
began at 8.30 in the morning and lasted till 6 P. M.
It was too dangerous to treat the patients by lamp-
light. It became necessary for the doctor to have
the following orders read out every morning:

1. Spitting near the doctor's house is strictly for-
   bidden.
2. Those who are waiting must not talk to each
   other loudly.
3. Patients and their friends must bring food
   enough for one day, as they cannot all be
   treated early in the day.
4. Anyone who spends the night on the station
   without the doctor's permission will be sent
   away without any medicine.
5. All bottles and tin boxes in which medicines
   are given must be returned.

As these orders were read out the natives nodded
vigorously to indicate that they understood and
then passed the word on to others so that the doctor's wishes might be made known in all the vil-
lages.

The natives named Dr. Schweitzer the
"Oganga," which means "fetishman." The
Negroes believed that any man who could cure
disease could also cause it by casting an evil spell
over his victims. That any disease should have a
natural cause never entered their minds. Every
trouble or misfortune, they believed, came from
some evil spirit.

A great deal of trouble was necessary to explain
how medicines were to be taken. Over and over
again the directions had to be read to them and

each time they solemnly repeated them, yet the doctor could never be sure that they would not empty the medicine on the ground, eat the ointment, and rub powders into their skins. On an average the doctor treated between thirty and forty patients a day and most of the sufferers were in great distress. The chief diseases were malaria, sleeping sickness, leprosy, elephantiasis, heart complaints, and dysentery.

Many people think that there is no toothache in such countries as Africa but Dr. Schweitzer found there was much acute suffering from decayed teeth. In some cases the victims suffered agonies but they were afraid of the polished forceps. They were amazed at the way in which the doctor could extract teeth. When some natives got artificial teeth, they were objects of envy, and many Negroes with perfectly good teeth wanted to have them drawn so that they might have new sets. There was little rest for Dr. Schweitzer, day or night. During the first nine months he treated nearly two thousand patients and he found nearly every disease that he had seen in Europe.

Once the doctor gained their confidence, the natives were not the least bit afraid of operations; in fact they used to quarrel as to who should submit to the knife first. The thing which amazed them more than anything else was the use of anæsthetics. How the doctor could put people to sleep and cut them open and then sew them up before the patient awakened seemed a miracle to them. One girl who had learned to write a little wrote to a friend at a distance: "Since Dr. Schweitzer came we have had the most wonderful things happen. First he kills the sick people, then he cures them, and after that he wakes them up again." One day a poor man, old and stricken with leprosy, rowed into Lambarene with his wife. He lived at Fernando Váz, two hundred and fifty miles away, but he had heard of the doctor and he and his wife had rowed the entire distance. It was little wonder that when he arrived he was so exhausted that he could scarcely stand.

The doctor worked under heavy handicaps. He had no proper buildings, nor had he sufficient medicines and bandages. He had to speak, especially at first, through an interpreter and he was dealing with poor people who were frightfully superstitious. In spite of these things the doctor fully enjoyed his work. Every day he was able to relieve suffering. Many who came to him in terrible pain left the mission house cured and in good health. Men and women and children came to him, plagued with sores, dragging their poor bleeding feet through the mud and suffering terrible agonies. Often after their sores had been properly treated and bandaged they leaped for joy and they could hardly restrain themselves.

The gratitude of the people was very touching. Sometimes they brought money hardly earned either by themselves or their relatives. One man, when he was cured, spent fourteen days at the mission making cupboards from old boxes. Another man insisted upon putting the roof of the doctor's house in good order so that when the rains came the building might be watertight. One man presented Mrs. Schweitzer with a valuable hippopotamus hide.

A common complaint among the natives is strangulated hernia, one of the most painful of all diseases. Nearly every day victims, nearly tortured into madness, would be brought to him. "Don't be afraid," the doctor would say kindly, "in an hour's time you shall be put to sleep, and when you wake you won't feel any more pain." The anæsthetic would soon be administered and the operation performed; then in a dimly lighted room the doctor would watch the sufferer's return to consciousness. Often the astonished patient would cry out: "I've no more pain! I've no more pain." He would feel for the doctor's hand and would not let it go. Incidents such as this happened every day and so it was that, in spite of hardship and loneliness, Dr. Schweitzer and his wife were happy beyond words. Often when sufferers for whom little could be done came to the doctor and told him of their sufferings, he found his own cheeks wet with tears.

After several years at Lambarene Dr. Schweitzer returned to Europe chiefly in order to arouse interest and raise money to carry on his work in Africa. Once again he used his great gifts as a musician and played upon some of the finest organs in Europe. Everywhere this truly great man was given a warm reception although many people declared that they could not understand why so great a musician and scholar should bury himself in the African jungle.

Dr. Schweitzer went back to Africa and to the poor people who so eagerly looked for his return. He has resumed his work among the black people of the jungle, for whom, even as a boy, he had tender sympathy. And so the world has lost a great musician, Strassburg University has lost a great scholar, but the poor suffering natives of the forest have restored to them a man whose love, sympathy, and humility is one of the miracles of modern life.

IV

WILLIAM PENN

Who Conquered Indians by Love

ON THE first day of September, 1682, a little
ship named the *Welcome* left the shores of
Old England and headed toward America. There
were one hundred emigrants on board, although
the severe hardships of the voyage thinned their
ranks before they reached their destination. An
ocean voyage in those days was a great undertaking. Sometimes when winds were unfavourable
the voyage lasted fourteen weeks, so a big stock
of provisions had to be taken. Here is a list of food-
stuffs taken by a vessel just at this time which
had just one hundred people on board: 32 fowl, 7
turkeys, 11 ducks, 2 lambs, a barrel of oranges, a
large keg of sweetmeats, a box of spices and one
of dried herbs, 18 coconuts, a box of eggs, 6 balls
of chocolate, and much solid food in the shape of
flour, sheep, and hogs. The *Welcome* must have
had a similar cargo so one can imagine what it
must have been like with the grunting of hogs, the

screaming of fowls, the baa-ing of sheep, the quacking of ducks. Add to all this the shouting of sailors and the anxious looks of the emigrants as they faced a new world and one gets a picture of the scene on board the *Welcome*. Nearly every day a passenger on board the *Welcome* died, and thirty persons were buried at sea.

The leader of the party was a Quaker named William Penn, a man in the prime of life. He left England because he had become thoroughly dissatisfied with conditions there. He resolved to found a colony where he could carry out his ideas of government and where he could enjoy the freedom of religious worship which had been denied him and his fellow Quakers in England. William Penn's father had been an admiral and the English king was under heavy obligations to him, one of these being a debt of eighty thousand dollars. That seemed a vast sum of money in those days and so when, after his father's death, William Penn offered to accept a piece of land in the New World in place of this money, the King agreed to Penn's proposal.

On October 27th the *Welcome* moored off the port of Newcastle in what is now the State of Delaware. Penn received a warm welcome from the white settlers who had been told beforehand of his hopes and ambitions for the new colony. A general holiday was proclaimed and the settlers, who were mostly Dutch, English, Swedes, and Germans, crowded around the landing place eager to catch a glimpse of this unusual man who was coming among them not so much as a lord and governor as a friend anxious to help everybody.

The next day Penn called all the people together at the courthouse and formerly took legal possession of the land. It was a strange gathering of settlers who had braved the hardships and rigours of a new and strange land that they might have freedom of worship and the chance to build up a new country. In addition to the whites, Indians came in their canoes and stood around wrapped in their fur robes and with tall waving feathers for headdress.

William Penn stood and faced them all. Slowly and solemnly he spoke and told them of his reasons for coming. Ever since he was a boy, he said, he had cherished the desire to found a free and virtuous democratic colony; where love and peace should reign and where the people should rule themselves. Solemnly he promised that every man should have liberty to follow the dictates of his conscience and should enjoy a share in the government of the state.

The people listened to his words with wonder and delight. They knew that Penn now owned all the surrounding country and, had he chosen, could lord it over them as others had done. These white men who had once lived in Europe knew how overbearing and harsh rich landowners could be. There was nothing of this about William Penn. Calling upon God to witness his vows he pledged himself to be their friend, to do justly, to love mercy, to walk humbly with God.

From the beginning Penn made a fine impression upon the Indians, who were the original possessors of the land. These Indians had suffered much at the hands of the white man. For generations their forefathers had wandered through the forests, untamed yet free. It is true they lived a precarious existence and spent much of their time in fighting, but they seldom received at the hands of the white man the consideration to which they were entitled.

That day when Penn addressed the colonists and Indians there was a lady present—Mrs. Preston—who lived to be over one hundred years old. Many years after that day, when she was a very old woman, she could still vividly remember the scene and often described it. She said that the Indians, as well as the whites, prepared the best entertainment that the place and circumstances permitted. Penn endeared himself to the Indians by his condescension. He walked with them, sat down on the ground with them, and ate with them of their roasted acorns and hominy. At this they expressed great delight and soon began to show how they could hop and jump. Then William Penn sprang up and, to cap the climax, beat them all at these games. The Indian warriors, both young and old, could scarcely restrain the extravagance of their joy.

As might have been expected there had been much bitter feeling between the Indians and the white men. Many bloody battles, often attended with terrible cruelty, had taken place, and even when they were at peace there was often suspicion and ill-concealed hatred. The native Indians resented the coming of these lordly white men who so often took away their hunting grounds and treated them with such contempt. Thus one bitter feud followed another and the Indians often smarted under a sense of injustice and sought revenge.

Penn decided to put an end to all this and so in November, 1682, before he had been among them a month, he invited the Indian chiefs and their warriors to meet him on the banks of the Delaware River and enter into a solemn covenant with him.

There was a natural amphitheatre which had been, for longer than anyone could remember, a

meeting place for the Indians. Here they held
solemn council, gravely settled their disputes, and
smoked the pipe of peace. This they had done for
ages before the palefaces came. It was named by
them "Sachamaxing," meaning "The Place of
Kings." At this spot was a magnificent elm tree,
over one hundred and fifty years old.

Under the great spreading branches of this beautiful old elm William Penn took his stand and
near him stood the leaders among the white settlers. He was now thirty-eight years of age with a
frank open face which radiated kindness and
honest sincerity. Mrs. Preston said he was the
most handsome man she had ever seen. The redskins, with waving plumes and bodies painted red,
yellow, and blue, seated themselves on the ground
in a half circle; the elders in front, the young warriors next, a number of Indian women with their
babies tied to them in the background. It was the
late fall season and the ground was covered with
brown leaves. Above were the lofty branches of
the elm, while in the centre the council fire burned.
The broad Delaware River flowed by and here
and there along its banks could be seen a log building standing in the midst of a clearing.

The reception over, Taminent, the great Indian
chief, took his place and announced to the governor that they were prepared to hear and consider

his words. Penn stepped forward and began his address to these sons of the forest. He reminded them that no matter how the palefaces and redskins might differ in appearance they were all children of the Great Spirit who wanted them to dwell in peace together. He told them that hatred and all bitterness were displeasing to God. "We have come to meet you," he said, "without guns or swords; with only good will and love in our hearts." He then submitted to them what he called "The Treaty of Friendship." This agreement proposed that they should live together as brothers; that all paths through the forest should be open and free; that the doors of the white men should be open to the redskins and the lodges of the Indians should be open to the white men. The treaty asked that they should not believe false reports about each other but should make careful inquiries before saying anything; that if a wrong were done, no one should seek revenge but should lay the case before a council of twelve honest men who would declare justice, and then the wrong would be buried in a pit which had no bottom. The treaty asked that the red men should assist the white men and the white men should help their red brothers; and that both the white men and the Indians should tell their children of this solemn treaty so that the loving friendship might grow stronger and be kept as long as the waters ran down the creeks and rivers and while the sun and moon and stars endured.

Penn's words made a deep impression upon all who heard them that day. When he finished the Indian chief advanced and took Penn's hand and the treaty was solemnly ratified. It was the first of its kind ever to be made in any country and—here is the important thing—it was kept. For although these redskins were seemingly wild and untrained men, they kept their vows and no drop of Quaker blood was ever shed by an Indian. Other white men had gone to the Indians with swords and guns, with the result that there had been cruel and bloody warfare, but when William Penn went to them with love, treating them as brothers, they instantly laid down their axes and tomahawks and treated the white man with the same love he had shown to them.

William Penn lived among the Indians for thirty-six years after that treaty was made and in all his dealings with them the Quaker governor showed the same peaceful, kindly spirit. Unfortunately many other white men did not act as he did. The custom of many, when dealing with the redskins, was to get them drunk and then cheat them. Others resorted to mean tricks such as using false weights and false maps. Such contemptible things Penn despised. He respected and loved the Indians and they knew it, and consequently they trusted him as few, if any, white men were ever trusted before by natives.

William Penn died on a morning of July, 1718, at the age of seventy-four. Perhaps the Indians felt his loss more than did any others. From far and near through the forest they came to bring presents and show sympathy to his widow. Not only the redskins but men everywhere hastened to pay their tribute of deep respect to one of the greatest men who ever lived. An eloquent man thus wrote of him: "The name of William Penn was cherished as a household word in the cottages of Wales and Ireland and among the peasantry of Germany; and not a tenant of a wigwam from the sea to the Susquehanna doubted his integrity. His fame is as wide as the world; he is one of the few who have gained abiding glory."

V

SIR JAMES YOUNG SIMPSON

Who Made Operations Painless

NEARLY a century ago a young medical student was present when an operation was being performed in a hospital. He was a sensitive young man with sympathies easily touched. As he watched the sufferings of the patient he said to himself over and over again, "Cannot something be done to render the patient unconscious while the operation is being performed, without interfering with the free and healthy play of the natural functions?"

This young doctor was James Young Simpson. He was born on June 7, 1811, at Bathgate, a village about twenty miles from Edinburgh, Scotland. His father was the village baker and James was the youngest of seven children.

There were two persons who exerted a great influence upon this sensitive boy. The first was the village schoolmaster. This man had a wooden leg and the boys nicknamed him "Timmerleg"

38

(timberleg). In spite of this handicap he was an excellent schoolmaster—far above the average—and he was quick to notice what a bright, intelligent boy James Simpson was. He did all he could to encourage him and to prepare him for college.

James had a really wonderful mother. When he became a man and saw any very earnest and energetic woman, his eyes would glisten with tears and he often said: "She reminds me of my mother." One day when he was small she noticed a hole in his stocking. There and then she took him on her knee and darned it. Then she surveyed her neatly executed work. "Jamie," she said, "when ye get to be a man and your mother's awa', remember that she was a grand darner."

James Young Simpson was only fourteen when he left his village home and enrolled as a student in arts at Edinburgh University. Later on he described his experience in these words: "I arrived in Edinburgh very young and very solitary, very poor and almost friendless." At first he was both downcast and homesick. After his native village Edinburgh seemed a very large city and he was an utter stranger. He even thought of returning home, but in his first year he won a scholarship worth fifty dollars annually which greatly encouraged him. He decided to become a doctor and in 1830 passed his final examination with honours, although he was scarcely out of his teens.

He was only twenty-six when he began his practice on the outskirts of Edinburgh. From the beginning there was no dearth of patients although most of them were quite poor. He also secured an appointment in a hospital and was soon working very hard. He succeeded so well that two years later he was appointed a professor in medicine at Edinburgh University. He quickly became famous as his unfailing courtesy and infinite patience inspired confidence. He was quite free from personal vanity and took as much pains with the poorest person as with the wealthy who also sought his services. In 1847 he was appointed one of Queen Victoria's physicians for Scotland.

He was now free to turn his attention to the subject which had been engrossing his attention for many years—the discovery of a safe anæsthetic. At this time surgical operations, besides being attended with great danger, were exceedingly painful. This pain was so great that surgical operations were only undertaken as a last resort—when everything else had failed. Even then many preferred to die rather than undergo the awful agony. The patient had to be strapped down to the table; he was hurriedly operated on by a surgeon whose nerves were raw with the thought of the terrible suffering he was causing. It was a ghastly undertaking from start to finish and it is no wonder that so many people preferred death.

Simpson was so moved at the sight of suffering that when a medical student he almost decided to give it up and try something else. He felt, however, that this would be playing the coward's part, so he decided to continue and to do all that he could to discover an anæsthetic for those who had to go under the surgeon's knife. In March, 1847, he read a paper before a group of outstanding medical men on this subject but, although they wished him success, few believed that he was likely to succeed.

In 1846 the news came from America that ether was being tried in surgery. It was as yet both dangerous and unsatisfactory but it was a step in the right direction and Simpson began to use it at once. Every spare moment he had he spent in the search for a real anæsthetic. He made scores of experiments with drugs and on more than one occasion he seriously endangered his life.

One day he called upon a friend of his, Dr. Lyon Playfair, who was a famous chemist. This man was experimenting with drugs in order to find an anæsthetic and so eager and trustful was Simpson that, there and then, he offered to inhale some of the vapour. Dr. Playfair refused to let him try until an experiment had been made upon two rabbits. Dr. Simpson chafed at what he thought was a waste of time, but the rabbits were treated. They lapsed into unconsciousness and later recovered. Simpson was delighted. The next day he suggested that he and his assistant should inhale the vapour. The assistant suggested, however, that before they did so they should find out how the two rabbits had fared. They did so and found that both rabbits were dead. Had the assistant not insisted on this precaution, undoubtedly both he and Simpson would have lost their lives.

Then came a great day for Simpson and, indeed, for the whole world. It was November 4, 1847. Simpson and his two assistants met to inhale possible new anæsthetics. Dr. Keith started to inhale half a small tumblerful. In two minutes he was under the dining-room table. Dr. Simpson and the other assistant, Dr. Duncan, soon followed him. If anyone had opened the door at that moment a very strange scene would have met their eyes, for the three doctors were lying helpless on the floor of the room. It so happened that Mrs. Simpson, her sister, and her niece did burst into the room soon after and were horrified at what they saw. Dr. Simpson was the first to regain consciousness. Very slowly he came to his senses and then he laughed aloud for joy. He knew that he had discovered something which would kill pain for thousands—literally for millions—of people. For years he had toiled day and night; he had experimented countless numbers of times, often at the risk of his life. But he had at last been rewarded. Here was an anæsthetic strong enough to render the patient quite unconscious and safe enough to be taken without danger.

Strange as it seems now, there were many who opposed the use of chloroform. Some people actually quoted the Bible to prove it was unnatural. But Dr. Simpson knew his Bible better than they did and silenced his objectors. Still the battle raged bitterly, but Queen Victoria took chloroform and Rev. Dr. Chalmers, one of the most famous clergymen of that time, favoured its use and eventually Dr. Simpson's discovery was hailed as a great boon. Just what this wonderful discovery has meant to mankind no one will ever know, but multitudes will never cease to thank God for Dr. Simpson and his gift to humanity.

Dr. Simpson himself became a victim to sciatica which caused him great pain. Yet he had marvellous will power and even when suffering acutely he continued to help others until he died. One day when he was suffering much and was about to seek relief by taking a steam bath, he remembered that he had neglected to see a patient whom he had promised to visit. He quickly dressed himself and, in spite of protests by his assistant, he risked a further chill in order to fulfil a promise he had made.

Dr. Simpson died on May 6, 1870. He was worn out by incessant labours for others. He admitted that he had not taken any vacation for several years and he was never "off duty." It was Queen Victoria's wish that he should be buried among the great in Westminster Abbey, but he had previously asked to be buried at Warriston near Edinburgh, the city he so loved and where he had laboured so long to relieve pain. Dr. Simpson did not live to see his sixtieth birthday, but he lived long enough to see the day when the most critical operations could be performed while the patients were blissfully unconscious of what was taking place. And if to give one's life in order to relieve ghastly pain is to be a hero, then surely a true hero sleeps in that grave at Warriston, overlooking Edinburgh.

VI

BENJAMIN FRANKLIN

Who Began Public Libraries in America

BENJAMIN FRANKLIN was born at Boston on January 6, 1706, and was one of a family of seventeen children. There were younger children but he was the youngest boy. Some of the children died in infancy but most of them lived to become men and women. Benjamin often sat down to his meals when, besides the father and mother, there were thirteen children present. With so many mouths to feed nothing could be wasted in that home; the most had to be made of every ounce of food and every article of clothing.

Benjamin's father, who was of English birth, was a tallow chandler and soap boiler. Education was not considered very necessary in those days and very few children attended school, a great many not at all. Benjamin was sent to school when he was eight and remained there for about two years. He learned to write fairly well but failed in arithmetic. When he was ten he was taken

destined to be his wife but neither he nor she dreamed of such a thing at that time.

Benjamin soon secured work as a printer. He was a good workman and very industrious. Again, whatever hardships he had known as a boy, being one of seventeen children had taught him to take care of his money, with the result that all through life he lived simply, never wasting his money on useless things. His industry was amazing. There was a good deal of drinking done at that time and many tradesmen spent hours in taverns while work was being neglected. Franklin drew up some rules by which to guide himself and he determined to spend no time foolishly. As a result he steadily gained the esteem of other citizens.

One day an important piece of printing had to be done and Benjamin, who was now in business for himself, was determined to do it satisfactorily. He worked hard all day and finished it, then by an accident, the type was spilled and scattered all over the floor. His day's hard work had gone for nothing. There and then he started to set it up again, working far into the night. A man named Dr. Baird happened to be going home late from his club and saw Franklin at work. He was greatly impressed by such industry and when, not long afterward, he heard some men say that Franklin's printing business would fail. he said: "You are wrong. The industry of Franklin is superior to anything I ever saw of the kind. I see him still at work when I go home from the club, and he is at work before his neighbours are out of bed."

He was sent to England to get better equipment for the printing business. He stayed there eighteen months, met some interesting people, and had many experiences which, while not altogether pleasant, certainly helped him in his business when he returned to Philadelphia. His mind was clearly made up on certain matters. In 1730 he published a newspaper, *The Gazette*, which was printed on better paper and with clearer type than any previously gotten out. He never allowed anything to be printed in it that was not true and well worth reading. He had often noticed sharp and deceitful methods of business practised by tradesmen. He knew these dishonest ways were not good for either the merchants or their customers, so he resolved that truth, sincerity, and integrity would mark all his dealings with men as long as he lived. He would always be fair and square and honest.

He further decided that he would never consider himself above doing honest work. As he prospered he was afraid that people might think him vain, so just to prove this was not so he used to bring home the paper he needed for his work in a wheelbarrow through the streets of the town. Other men, not so well off as he, would have scorned such a thing, but honest work, said Franklin, was nothing to be ashamed of, and his modesty and industry created a favourable impression.

About 1740, Franklin and his friends used to meet regularly at the home of a Mr. Grace and discuss the few books and magazines they had read. At this time books were very scarce. There was only one bookshop in America and that was in Boston. People who wanted books had generally to send all the way to England for them. Of course such a convenience as a public library was unknown. Franklin proposed to his friends that they should bring what books they had to Mr. Grace's home where they would form a common library which could be consulted at any time. All agreed to this, and while the library did not take up more than one end of a small room, it must have seemed quite a collection to them, and they were proud of it.

A year or two later Franklin proposed the commencement of a subscription library. He carefully drew up a number of rules for conducting it and managed to secure fifty subscribers at forty shillings each. There was to be an annual fee of ten shillings. A charter was secured and soon the number of subscribers rose to one hundred. This was the first subscription library and the mother of all such institutions on the American continent, and it was due solely to the forethought and tireless patience of Benjamin Franklin.

He interested himself in a great many other things which were for the public good. He formed a club to meet every Friday evening which became known as the Junta. One rule was that every member in turn should discuss some subject which the other members would consider. In a time of so few books and papers these discussions were of great value to those who took part, and this club continued its regular meetings for nearly *forty years*. It was doubtless one of the best and most useful clubs of its kind ever conducted. Any member who, during discussion, lost his temper was fined, with the result that lessons of fair play and good will were learned by all.

Probably there never was a man who worked harder for the public good than Benjamin Franklin. It was through his efforts that the streets of Philadelphia were paved and cleaned and lighted for the first time, with such pleasing results that the custom spread to other cities. He was responsible for having trees planted in the streets, thus greatly improving their appearance. He studied ways to prevent houses being burned—fires were very frequent in those days—and he founded the first fire insurance company in North America. For the comfort of householders he invented a stove which became known as the "Franklin stove," which is still in use to-day. In a time when education was very hard to get he founded an academy which later became the University of Pennsylvania. When a citizen of Philadelphia, Dr. Bond, was trying to get a hospital erected and was meeting ridicule and opposition, Franklin approved of the plan and supported him. Indeed there does not seem to have been any movement for the public good in which Franklin did not have a hand.

As he became old, many well-deserved honours came to him. He was one of a committee to draw up the Declaration of Independence and although he was over seventy he was elected to Congress. He was, even at his advanced age, elected First Minister to the Court of France and Governor of the State of Pennsylvania. One of the last things this truly noble and public-spirited man did was to sign a memorial to Congress asking for the abolition of slavery.

Franklin died on April 17, 1790, at the age of eighty-four. Even on his deathbed he was making plans to help others. It is little wonder that it was said of him: "Such a servant, citizen, and patriot no other country ever had in the history of man."

VII

GEORGE WASHINGTON GOETHALS

Who Did What Seemed Impossible

ABOUT sixty years ago there was a boy living in Brooklyn, New York, who after school hours each day hurried away to his work as a cashier in a New York market. He did this from the time he was eleven years old, as his parents needed the money and he wanted to help them. He was a cheerful, good-natured lad, and although he had to work each evening and on Saturdays while his chums were playing games, he did not grouch or get sorry for himself. "My parents need the money," he said, "and I need the education." In this way George Washington Goethals supported himself while at school.

Still working each evening, he entered college and began to study to be a doctor, but the long hours of study and work told on his health and he had to give up that idea. In 1876, when he was eighteen, he entered West Point Academy and began to study army engineering. From the beginning he was a popular student and before graduation was elected president of his class. He was eager to learn and never thought himself above doing anything his instructors asked him to do. "I came here to learn," he used to say.

His willingness to work and his efficiency brought him to the attention of Mr. W. H. Taft, who was at that time Secretary of War. In 1905 Mr. Taft found it necessary to inspect the work being done on the Panama Canal and to make plans for fortifying it. He took George W. Goethals—who by this time had been promoted to the rank of major—along with him.

It was generally recognized that the building of the Panama Canal was one of the greatest engineering feats which had ever been attempted, but could it be successfully carried out? That was a question which people everywhere were asking. There were many capable and experienced men who said frankly that it could not be done.

The great French engineer, Ferdinand de Lesseps, builder of the Suez Canal, had undertaken to construct the Panama Canal but after two hundred and fifty million dollars had been spent the work scarcely had been begun and De Lesseps, broken-hearted, was compelled to give up. Mr. Roosevelt and Mr. Taft both had sufficient confidence in Goethals to believe that he

could succeed where others had failed. "But the
only way he can do it," said Roosevelt, "is by
taking full management and staying at the Canal
all the time."

In 1907 Goethals was put in charge of the
Panama Canal and it remained to be seen if he
could succeed where others had failed. He knew
perfectly well that he had tackled one of the
hardest jobs that any man ever undertook. In the
first place, the climate was a serious handicap, for
chiefly through lack of proper sanitation, hundreds of workmen had died. These men were of so
many different nationalities that trouble broke
out continually. A passage nine miles long had to
be made through the mountain rock at what is
now called the "Culebra Cut." The rock seemed
like granite and offered stubborn resistance to the
great army of workmen who, armed with huge
drills and picks, swarmed around the rocks carv-
ing a way through the mountain. Day after day
for months and even years, tremendous explosions
of dynamite were necessary to split rocks asunder,
then, after the explosion, tons of earth had to be
shovelled away. "We have to fight against nature,"
said Goethals, and the hard, stiff battle went on
for years. Sometimes it almost seemed as if the
resistance offered by mountains and rocks would
be too great even for so determined and patient an

engineer as Goethals. Later someone remarked
that Goethals removed a mountain from the
landscape just as easily as other men moved a
saltcellar on their dining table. But this was not
so, for while he never lost his confidence Goethals
had many anxious hours.

For years he had under him not less than forty
thousand men, speaking forty-five different lan-
guages. He was responsible for seeing that they
were all properly housed and fed; for keeping up
enormous supplies of machinery and tools and,
what was the hardest task of all, keeping everybody in good humour and satisfied. He succeeded
in doing these things; never was an employer more
popular with his men. They liked his modesty.
Although he was a colonel in the army he never
wore his uniform while in Panama and gave himself no overbearing airs. He was patient and good-
natured, with a keen sense of humour, and his
men enjoyed that. Then he believed that the Canal
could be built and his confidence spread to all
around him with the result that every man went
to work with a will inspired by his fine example.
Furthermore, every man knew that there was no
harder worker on the Canal than Colonel Goethals
himself. He was up early and late, and there was
no detail that escaped his attention and no advice
he was not willing to give. "The only time that

the Colonel isn't working," said one foreman, "is between ten P. M. and five A. M. and then he is asleep."

The heat was often terrific and, of course, with so much machinery pounding away, the noise was deafening. Holes cannot be bored through great mountains without noise, yet Goethals stayed on the job for seven years and set an example of hard work and perseverance which has seldom been equalled and which inspired the workmen to do their best.

There were so many vexed problems to solve and disputes to settle that Goethals established what may be called a "court." He sat at his desk at what he used laughingly to call the "Throne Room," and here every imaginable kind of case was brought before him. Some people would be dissatisfied with their living quarters; others had been injured and wanted compensation; a great many wanted their wages raised, while family quarrels were constantly being aired. Goethals was not a lawyer but he had a way of settling disputes that somehow seemed to make everybody feel better.

"All work and no play makes Jack a dull boy." Colonel Goethals realized this and he knew that recreation was necessary for men as well as boys. He saw that provision was made for all manner of games both indoor and outdoor. Basketball, football, bowling, baseball, and other games were all made possible, and good equipment supplied; reading rooms with books, magazines, and newspapers were provided. The women who were brave enough to live down in Panama with its dangers and monotony were not forgotten and first-class band concerts and other fine entertainments were arranged. These things all proved well worth while and the result was forty thousand contented workmen, every man anxious to do his best. "He's the squarest boss I ever worked for," said one workman to a visitor, and that is how the entire Panama gang felt about their "boss." It is well known that Colonel Goethals frowned upon graft and dishonesty of every kind. Honest and straightforward himself, he would not tolerate dishonesty in others. From the time he took charge of the great task until he finished it he was determined to make it a clean job and in this high purpose he was successful.

One of the hardest fights that Colonel Goethals had was against disease. For years workmen had died at an alarming rate; some dry seasons they had died like flies. It was largely due to the determination of Goethals to make Panama a reasonably safe place in which to live that the menace of disease was greatly reduced. He carried through a fine system of sanitation and engaged the best medical advice possible to insure the safety and comfort of the workmen and their families.

The great day came in September, 1913. In spite of the misgivings of his friends and the doleful prophecies of adverse critics the Panama Canal was completed; the first ship sailed safely through Gatun Locks and the Canal was thrown open to the ships of the world. Letters and telegrams of congratulation came to Colonel Goethals from all parts of the world; he had succeeded where others had failed, and many who had often said that the Canal would never be constructed were the first to acknowledge themselves in the wrong and to offer their hearty congratulations.

As a boy George W. Goethals had been shy and retiring; as a man, successful as few other men in history have been successful, he remained modest and unspoiled. Honours came to him from universities and societies; he was loaded with medals and degrees and greeted by admiring crowds. But where most other men would have been in their glory he was plainly embarrassed by so much admiration. "It is awful," he said.

One thing he made clear: he was not solely responsible for the success of the entire project. He could not forget the thousands of others, whether foremen or labourers, who had worked hard. He spoke of the doctors and nurses who had fought disease. He remembered the women who had braved climatic dangers and stayed with their husbands year after year. When given a medal from the National Geographic Society, he said: "In accepting this medal, and thanking those who confer it, I do so in the name of every member of the Canal army." And this modest and capable man, who began life so humbly, successfully completed what must be regarded as one of the greatest engineering feats of all history.

VIII

LOUIS PASTEUR

A Physician to the Whole Human Race

JUST two days after Christmas Day, 1822, a boy was born in France who was destined to become a great fighter. His father, Joseph Pasteur, had been a soldier in Napoleon's army, and when Napoleon was defeated and his men were ordered to throw down their arms Joseph Pasteur refused. An Austrian officer was so impressed by Pasteur's determination that he allowed him to keep his sword. Louis Pasteur, the son, became a fighter in another sense. He was equally brave and even more determined than his father, but he fought against disease and pain in such a way that all the world gratefully remembers him.

When he was sixteen Louis was sent from his home in the country to an academy in the great city of Paris. He had never been away from home before and the loneliness was too much for him. He became very homesick and soon had to return to his people. He attended a school in a near-by town and soon outstripped all the other pupils, not because he was naturally cleverer than they were—in fact he often failed in different subjects —but because whatever he attempted he tackled with all his might. There were boys in that school quicker to learn than Louis Pasteur but there was no boy so determined to master his lessons.

Soon after, he began to study medicine and he put his whole heart into it. At that time surgery was little more than in its beginnings. Out of every ten persons who underwent an operation no less than *six died*. In a great many of the old hospitals the equipment was so poor that a patient's chance of recovering after an operation was very slim indeed. Thousands of people were so afraid of the surgeon's knife that they preferred to die of their ailments than go to a surgeon. "What is the use of being cut by the knife?" they said; "almost everybody dies after the operation."

It was not during the operation, or immediately after it, that these sufferers generally died, but often many weeks later. Blood poisoning, gangrene, erysipelas, and other infections nearly always attacked the patient even when the operation seemed to have been quite satisfactory. At that time practically everybody—doctors included—held that germs developed of themselves wherever there had been disease. Wise men had believed this for hundreds of years. They saw through powerful microscopes that millions of germs soon appeared wherever there was decay and fermentation, so they concluded that these living things originated in the diseased parts. How else, they asked, could these germs—which had a million descendants in forty-eight hours—be explained? And nobody cared to question what had been believed by scientists for many centuries.

Pasteur arrived at the conclusion that the germs came from disease-laden air and that if wounds were properly dressed and—still more important —if all the physicians' instruments were thoroughly sterilized, the germs would not get to the patient and kill him.

Pasteur arrived at his conclusion after making many painstaking experiments and showing infinite patience. At first he was laughed at for his pains and leading medical men asked him to prove his position. This he did successfully by several demonstrations, and, to the credit of his opponents it must be said that they freely acknowledged themselves in the wrong and welcomed Pasteur's discovery as one of the greatest in the history of medicine. His careful instructions have been followed ever since by physicians everywhere with the result that surgical infection is practically a thing of the past; untold suffering has been prevented and hundreds of thousands of lives have been saved.

On one occasion the Minister of Agriculture in France called upon Pasteur and asked his aid in a very important matter. One of the chief industries of France was that of silk production. A mysterious disease had settled upon the silkworms in France, and the thousands of people who depended upon this industry for a livelihood were in great distress and despair. Pasteur immediately set out to help these people. He established a laboratory in the silk-growing district and for four years toiled unceasingly to arrest this disease. During this time his father passed away and soon afterwards his daughter died. These were heavy blows to a sensitive, home-loving man like Pasteur but he never slackened his efforts until he had arrested the silkworm disease and he had the satisfaction of seeing the industry completely restored. His magnificent work saved the country thirty million francs a year. For a time he was worn out by his labours. He had a stroke of paralysis and it seemed as if this extraordinary man, so unselfish and so eager to help others, would die. He made an unexpected recovery, however, and in a year or two he was working as hard as ever.

A disease called anthrax attacked the cattle of

France and once again Pasteur's services were sought. He experimented over and over while many of the greatest scientists of Europe, some of whom were very critical, looked on. He believed that by inoculating cattle with doses of anthrax the disease could be overcome. It was decided to make a test before a group of medical authorities.

Fifty sheep were injected with virulent doses of anthrax. Of this number twenty-five were given Pasteur's treatment from the beginning and the other twenty-five were treated in the customary way. Within four days every one of the latter group was dead while not one of those treated by Pasteur died. Never was an experiment more successful. It was a complete victory for Pasteur and his critics were silenced.

Pasteur now turned his attention to a disease which had become a terrible scourge in France and in many other countries, hydrophobia, a disease caused by the bite of a mad dog. Up to the time he began his researches practically the only method of treatment was to cauterize the wound within half an hour of its infection. This treatment, besides being exceedingly painful, was very unsatisfactory and thousands of persons, mostly children, died from hydrophobia every year.

All his life Louis Pasteur had wished there was a cure for this disease. When he was nine years old a mad wolf had visited the countryside where he lived and filled everybody with terror. It had bitten men and beasts, all of whom died. He had seen a poor peasant named Nicole, who had been bitten by the wolf, cauterized with a red-hot iron at the smithy near his father's house. He never forgot these things and so he began to search for some way to combat this terrible disease.

Whenever he heard of a dog going mad he hurried to the scene to get some of the saliva which was so poisonous from its mouth in order to study it under the microscope. Once he risked his life in this way. He had a tube placed in the mouth of a mad dog and with the other end between his lips he actually drew some of the poisonous saliva up into the tube by the suction of his own breath. He took a great chance but he secured the saliva and then hurried off with it to the laboratory to examine it and experiment with it.

After many experiments he found that if a certain amount of serum were injected into the body it would give a person hydrophobia. He believed, however, that if a person had a weak serum already in his blood it would be an antiseptic and the disease could not be taken. He took a number of rabbits and gave them a weak serum regularly for several days, then he gave them each a strong dose—enough to kill an ordinary rabbit.

But they were immune to the disease because of the serum already taken. Of course there was still the question as to whether this would work in the same way with human beings. He was soon to find out.

One day in October, 1885, six shepherd lads were watching the sheep near their mountain home in Jura when a mad dog with foaming jaws rushed into the meadow and attacked them. The boys fled and the eldest of them, named Juliffe, turned to protect his friends. The dog rushed at him and fastened its teeth upon his left hand. The boy wrestled with the infuriated animal and a terrific struggle took place. Juliffe's little brother ran back and managed to lash the dog's jaws together with a whip thong.

Juliffe's life was saved for the time being but he was fearfully bitten and mauled. Everybody feared that he would die from hydrophobia but the mayor of the little town said he believed that if he were taken to Paris, the great Louis Pasteur could save his life. The boy, suffering much, was brought to Pasteur but the scientist hesitated. He had only tried his method with one person previously—a little Alsatian boy of ten—and the experiment was a success. Should he try again? He decided to do so and Juliffe was inoculated with the serum. For more than two weeks it seemed uncertain as to whether the boy would recover or not. Through the long hours of each night Pasteur could not sleep. He was torn with anxiety. When the boy took a change for the better and Pasteur realized that the experiment was successful his joy was unbounded as he knew now that the terrible scourge could be conquered. As a result of what he discovered the death rate from hydrophobia has now been reduced to one in a hundred. In the first four months after his discovery, out of three hundred and fifty persons who were inoculated, only one life was lost. These two boys, the ten-year-old Alsatian boy and Juliffe, were the first of a vast number whose lives have been saved as a result of Pasteur's devoted labours.

As he grew older a great many honours came to Louis Pasteur for he made many other discoveries. He was referred to by a distinguished man as: "The most perfect man who ever entered the Kingdom of Science." The French Government awarded him and his family a generous pension and he was made Chevalier of the Legion of Honour. He was elected to the American National Association of Sciences. In 1888 the great Pasteur Institute was opened in Paris and liberal contributions for its erection and maintenance came from all over the world.

Pasteur was a very kind and sympathetic man

and he cared little for some things which would have pleased others. He lived to do good, to check disease, to fight pain and suffering. He cared nothing about personal gain and always lived very simply.

On Saturday afternoon, September 28, 1895, he passed peacefully away surrounded by friends and members of his family. Thus ended a beautiful life, a life so unselfish and loving that it must ever be an inspiration to others.

IX

ALEXANDER GRAHAM BELL

WHO GAVE WINGS TO WORDS

ONE day in 1870 a young man twenty-three years of age and in delicate health stood in the consulting room of a physician in Edinburgh, Scotland. "You are far from well," said the doctor, "there is only one hope for you. If you seek a climate less severe than this one, and live outdoors, you may regain your health."

The young man was Alexander Graham Bell. Not long before this two of his brothers had died of tuberculosis and it seemed as if he also were to become a victim of the disease. His father was determined to give his boy every possible chance. "I will take him to Canada," he said; "he can live in the clear air there and help around the farm; perhaps he may become healthy."

The Bells moved to a farm near Brantford, Ontario, and soon Alexander's health was greatly improved. Many hours each day he spent out in the fields, ploughing and planting, and his father was especially delighted at the improvement in his health. Alexander himself was contented and whistled as he worked.

Before he left Scotland, Alexander Bell had become greatly interested in efforts being made to help deaf people understand what others were saying by watching their lip movements. His mother was deaf and his father, who was a fine elocutionist, had begun a method of teaching the deaf and dumb to read what was called "visible speech."

Before he could read a note of music Alexander Bell would often sit at the piano and play well by ear, so well, indeed, that many thought him an accomplished musician. This quick ear for sound was destined to be of great value to him later on. Several years before he left his home in Scotland he was experimenting with the laws of sound.

One day, when listening to the sound made by the vibration of a tuning fork, he asked himself why sound could not be made to travel along a copper wire and be heard at a considerable distance away. At first he thought only of making musical notes travel; the idea of having the human voice carried along the wires came to him later.

While Alexander worked on the farm in Ontario his father had been asked to give some lessons at a school for deaf and dumb children in Boston. The authorities were delighted with his work and pressed him to remain. "I cannot accept your offer," he said, "but I have a son in Ontario who understands my methods and can teach these children as well as I can."

An offer was made to Alexander which he promptly accepted, and he began to teach in the Boston school at a salary of five hundred dollars a year. His success with the deaf mutes greatly astonished the school authorities and news of what he was doing spread through the whole country-side.

One day a great man visited Boston. This was Dom Pedro, Emperor of Brazil, who was visiting the United States in order to learn all he could about whatever he thought would help his people. He was greatly interested in what Alexander Bell was doing for the deaf mutes and spent a con-siderable time with him, asking a great many questions and freely expressing his admiration. Meanwhile Alexander Bell kept working away at his invention every spare moment he had. He firmly believed that it was possible to make sound travel along wires and he was determined to find out how to do it.

A man named Sanders, who lived at Salem, near Boston, brought a five-year-old boy, who was deaf and dumb, to Bell with the pathetic request that something be done to help him. Mr. Sanders suggested that Alexander Bell should live in their home in exchange for giving the boy lessons and Bell accepted the offer. This man was greatly interested in the efforts of the young inventor and let him have the use of his cellar for experimenting. So hour after hour he laboured trying to make sound travel. Sometimes he seemed on the verge of discovery, then a difficulty would arise which might have discouraged him had he not been so patient and determined. He stretched wire from the house to the barn and tried to send messages. Whenever he noticed any improvement he would become greatly excited and, as Mr. Sanders said, "He leaped like an Indian in a war dance."

One day a Boston lawyer named Hubbard brought his fifteen-year-old girl Mabel, who was quite deaf, to Bell and asked him to teach her. Like Mr. Sanders, this man became greatly interested in Bell's attempts to make sound travel and the two men supplied him with money in order that he might work at his invention. These two were very kind and generous to Bell but sometimes they thought he was only a dreamer and that his ideas were not very practical. However, they did give him considerable encouragement and this meant a great deal to Bell, as most people who knew what he was trying to do said frankly that he was wasting both time and money; that his hopes were doomed to utter failure. But day after day he went on experimenting, evidently believing in himself and not discouraged by ridicule or opposition.

A friend of his who was an ear specialist secured for him the ear of a dead person and after many careful experiments he succeeded in making the sound of his voice travel from the drum of this ear along a delicate straw. He said to himself: "Why could not a very fine, sensitive iron plate take the place of this eardrum and why could not copper wire take the place of this straw?"

At this time Mr. Sanders and Mr. Hubbard became persuaded that the invention was impossible and refused to give him any further help. This was a severe blow to Bell as he was almost penniless. The outlook seemed dark indeed. He had applied to Washington for a patent for his invention and he received a letter summoning him there. Mr. Sanders loaned him enough to pay his fare and off Bell went. While in Washington he called upon a distinguished scientist and electrician, Professor Joseph Henry, and showed him the instrument he had so far developed. Very carefully the old scientist examined the instrument while the young inventor awaited the verdict with his heart in his mouth. At last the professor spoke: "You have made a beginning on a marvellous invention," he said. "Do not stop until it is finished." These words gave Bell, who was just twenty-eight years old, a tremendous thrill. "I will never give up," he said. When Mr. Sanders and Mr. Hubbard heard what the scientist had said they were greatly pleased and agreed to supply him with the money to continue his experiments.

In order to get certain delicate instruments made Bell went to an electrical shop where he formed an acquaintance with a young man named Thomas Watson. This man was keenly interested in Bell's invention and the two spent a great many hours together, as Watson's electrical knowledge was useful to the inventor. Bell did succeed in making sound travel over wire but for many months there was nothing distinct; there were simply noises. Over and over he tried, each time using instruments more delicate and sensitive. He perfected the diaphragm using goldbeater's skin, which is very much like the human ear. Opposite to it he set up an electromagnet through which the electric current passed over the wire. Then, one day in June, 1875, he managed to pass the twang of a watch spring over the wire and he was wild with excitement. Still there was much yet to be done and more months of tremendous concentration and hard work were necessary. Then came a never-to-be-forgotten day.

It was March 10, 1876. Bell was in one room with his instrument and Watson was at the end of the wire in another room. Suddenly Watson heard Bell's voice over the wire say distinctly: *"Mr. Watson, please come here, I want you."* The telephone had been discovered. True, it was by no means perfect, and even simple sentences had often to be repeated five or six times before the meaning could be understood. But the beginning was made and one of the most useful and marvellous inventions of all time was born.

Alexander Bell was granted the patent for his wonderful invention on his twenty-ninth birthday but it was some considerable time before its value was recognized. In 1876 there was a great Centennial Exposition in Philadelphia; substantial prizes were being given for new inventions and many remarkable things such as the first electric light, the first reaper and binder, and other things were on view and competition was keen. Bell was anxious that his "Baby Telephone" should be considered by the judges. He was, however, unfortunate in not being able to secure a good position. While other inventions were displayed to advantage, the best Bell could do was to have a small table in a corner, and it looked as if the judges would never even see his telephone. All day these men passed from one place to another carefully considering each invention in turn. It was seven o'clock in the evening before they passed near Bell and they were impatient to be through. He was given a chance to explain his device but they were bored. Some of them openly laughed at his idea of making the human voice travel. But Dom Pedro, Emperor of Brazil, was with the judges and he spoke up and told of Bell's great success with deaf mutes. This secured from him a better hearing. Bell spoke to the Emperor: "Put your ear to this receiver," he said. Dom Pedro did so and Bell went to the far end of the room and began to talk over the wire. Astonishment, then amazement, spread over Dom Pedro's face. "My God! It talks!" he fairly shouted. Then Professor Henry, who had encouraged Bell some time before, took up the receiver and he was equally astonished. The judges now changed their attitude and stayed for hours examining the new discovery. The next day they gave their decision that the telephone was the most wonderful of all the exhibits. Many people were hard to convince and insisted that there was a trick somewhere and that the invention was a fraud, but at last even this criticism disappeared.

Soon afterward the Bell Telephone Company was organized and in the first eight years paid dividends amounting to over four million dollars. The telephone spread to other lands and in less than twenty-five years it was being used in nearly every civilized country in the world.

Alexander Bell became a wealthy man. He married Mabel Hubbard, the deaf mute of whose education he had charge for many years when she was a girl.

For many years he continued to perfect his invention and he lived to see his discovery made a means of blessing to millions. He used to spend his summers in Cape Breton, Nova Scotia, and there he died in 1922, having given to the world a priceless means of communication.

GEORGE WASHINGTON CARVER

Who Saw the Great Value of Common Things

IN 1894 a young Negro was attending Iowa State College and supporting himself by doing laundry work, helping in the greenhouses, and working at any other odd jobs by which he could help to pay his way. He had already put himself through high school by doing with all his might whatever honest work he could find, and his record as a student and as a worker was something of which any boy might be proud.

This boy was born in Missouri of parents who were slaves. When he was a baby he and his mother were seized and carried off by unscrupulous persons. He never knew what happened to his mother but he was rescued and brought up by a family named Carver who were very kind to him. He was known by their name and as he was especially truthful, the name of the first American President was added; so the little black boy became known as George Washington Carver. The

lad knew nothing of his father except that he had
been a slave and met an accidental death one day
when he was hauling wood.

George did not get an opportunity to attend
school during the first ten years of his life. His
only book was a speller and this well-thumbed
volume he knew by heart. When he was ten he
had his first chance to go to school and he was
glad to get it. By this time he had left the Carvers
and had to support himself while at school by
working for families in their kitchens and making
himself generally useful in doing almost every
kind of housework. He had a very hard struggle
and only a brave boy could have come through
successfully. Once he began a week with only ten
cents. He bought five cents' worth of corn meal,
and five cents' worth of suet, and on what he made
out of this he lived for a whole week. He was willing to tackle almost any kind of work in order to
keep at school and pay his way, and eventually he
reached college.

When George Carver was at Iowa State College
that wonderful leader of his people, Booker T.
Washington, saw him and was at once greatly
attracted to him. He offered him a position as a
teacher in Tuskegee Institute, Alabama, where
thousands of young Negroes have been given fine
training. Carver had by this time gained a Master

of Arts degree with an exceptionally fine standing and was well fitted for the position. He accepted it and soon began his work at Tuskegee.

When George Carver went to Tuskekee he found the condition of the large Negro population in Alabama very discouraging. A few years before this Booker T. Washington had travelled hundreds of miles through Alabama closely observing the life of the Negro people. Most of the travelling was done over very bad roads and in old buggies drawn by mules. Most of the people lived in small cabins. He found that as a rule the whole family slept in one room. Often, in addition to the family, relatives or visitors shared the cabin. There was very rarely any place to bathe and often there wasn't even provision for washing one's face and hands. The usual diet of the people was fat pork and corn bread. Seldom did the family sit down together for a meal. The husband would take his bread and meat in his hand and start for the field, eating as he walked. In one corner of the room his wife would be seated eating her meal while the children ran in and ate what they could get as they came from the yard.

The one object seemed to be to plant cotton and frequently it was growing right up to the cabin doors. Everybody seemed to go to the field and every child that was old enough to carry a hoe was put to work, and the baby would be laid down at the end of the cotton row so that the mother could give it some attention when she had finished chopping her row. In the cabins there were ornamental clocks, most of which did not keep time, and even when they did there was no one in the cabin who could tell the time of day. Often there would be an organ that no one could play.

It was the ignorance of the poor people which deeply moved both Booker T. Washington and George Carver. As a rule the schools were miserably poor and the teachers were seldom able to teach much. Often four or five pupils would be studying from one book and in many schools there wasn't even a blackboard.

George W. Carver, who was now Professor Carver, quickly decided that the best way to help the people was to teach them how to get the most out of the soil. The ground and the climate were both good enough to give the people a decent living, if they were taught what to grow and how to grow it. There were millions of Negroes living a miserable hand-to-mouth existence and blaming the land for being so poor, when they did not even begin to understand how many different crops the soil could sustain and the varied uses to which these things could be put.

Professor Carver found after much careful

scientific research that the sweet potato, which grew in abundance throughout the whole countryside, could be put to a great many uses. This is what Margaret R. Seebach writes in *The Land of All Nations:* "He (George Carver) has succeeded in making four varieties of flour, five kinds of library paste, three kinds of breakfast foods, two kinds of coffee, fourteen varieties of candy, forty-five dyes ranging from jet-black to a rich orange; as well as starch, vinegar, ink, shoe blacking, molasses, fillers for wood; and substances resembling coconut, chocolate, tapioca, preserved ginger, and a rubber which may prove to be his most valuable invention. Thus, from sweet potatoes alone, over a hundred products have been derived in his laboratory, each and all of which can be readily manufactured for practical use."

The peanut is another crop easily raised in the soil of Alabama and here again Professor Carver, after careful and thorough study, found possibilities of which no one had even dreamed. Who would think that the lowly peanut was of much value? Yet the list of uses to which it can be put is a most astonishing one. Soon millions of Negroes were taught to realize that the hitherto despised peanut crops were able to make them comfortable and even rich, and enable them to lift up their heads with a sense of independence and self-respect.

From his experiments with the pecan nut Carver was able to develop more than sixty products among which were rope, carpeting, baskets, matting, and ribbon.

It was one thing for Professor Carver to make these scientific discoveries; it was another thing for him to stir up the people and get the information to them. It is to his credit that he freely placed his knowledge in the hands of the people who so pathetically needed it, and that he did not seek to make himself rich by his discoveries. His own terrible struggle up from childhood; his almost heartbreaking attempts to secure work when he was putting himself through high school and college; the prejudice he had often met, all made him willing and eager to help his people. Once he himself had applied by mail for admission to a college in Iowa and his application was accepted, but when he appeared and the teachers saw he was a Negro he was turned away at once.

There are twelve millions of his people in the United States and the sad conditions under which many of them were living made a tremendous appeal to George Carver, as they did to Booker T. Washington, and the only payment he has sought is the satisfaction of knowing that he has helped many thousands of them to self-respect and independence and usefulness.

He has personally spoken to hundreds of gatherings of his people, carefully explaining his ideas, and sparing himself no labour in order to get them interested. Not content with this, he has written many pamphlets, which have been published by the Tuskegee Institute and widely circulated. Among these are: *How To Grow the Peanut and 105 Ways of Preparing It for Human Use; How to Grow the Tomato and 115 Ways of Preparing It for the Table; How to Make Sweet Potato Flour, Starch, Sugar, Bread and Mock-Coconut; Possibilities of the Sweet Potato in Macon County, Alabama; How to Dry Fruits and Vegetables; Increasing the Yield of Corn,* and *When, What and How to Preserve Fruits and Vegetables in the Home.* It is no exaggeration to say that, as a result of his painstaking scientific discoveries, George W. Carver has made a much higher standard of living possible to thousands if not millions of his people.

Other people besides the Negroes have not been slow to recognize his work and to show their appreciation of it. He was made a Fellow of the Royal Society of Arts in London, an honour which comes to very few men; but it was gladly given to this Negro. In 1922 he was awarded the Spingarn Medal which is given to: "That man or woman of African descent and American citizenship who shall have made the highest achievement during the preceding year or years in any honourable field of human endeavour." Other distinctions have come to him all of which he has borne modestly and each one of which has made him anxious to do even more for the people who already are so greatly indebted to him.

One day a young Negro student at Tuskegee came to Professor Carver and asked him if he might have the use of a classroom on Sunday. Permission was granted and the next Sunday Professor Carver looked in and found three men studying the Bible. Next day these men told him that they had formed a Bible Class and elected him as teacher. He tried to get out of it but they insisted and this already overworked man consented. He has taught that Bible Class for many years. It has grown greatly in numbers and in usefulness, for here, as with everything else he does, George Carver never does a thing carelessly. He thinks that if a thing is worth doing at all, it is worth doing well.

There is still poverty and ignorance among millions of Negroes of the South, as there is among many other peoples, but a very great improvement has been effected during recent years. Better and more sanitary homes have been built; schools and churches and libraries have been erected. Life for thousands has been completely changed and much of the credit for all this must be placed to the credit of a modest but tremendously patient and hard-working Negro—George Washington Carver.

tobacco smoke and the songs and jests were the coarsest that evil imaginations could conceive.

Four years before he went to London, George Williams had decided to become a Christian and he joined the church. When he went to the great city he was well aware that he would find it much harder to live up to his ideals there than in the little country town where he had spent his apprenticeship, but he was a determined lad and once he made up his mind to do a thing he did not readily give up. He also signed a temperance pledge promising to remain a total abstainer, a brave and difficult thing to do at that time.

George got on remarkably well both with his employers and the young men with whom he was associated. He was not afraid of hard work. He was courteous and obliging, willing and eager to help anyone he could, and not disposed to quarrel. No matter how the other young fellows might differ from him in their habits of living—and many of them certainly differed a great deal— they were all ready to admit that George Williams was a decent and likable fellow, one of the most popular of the one hundred and forty assistants who worked for the firm. Even when promotion and steady advancement came to him there was never any sign of spite or envy shown by his associates.

George Williams began to invite serious-minded young fellows to his bedroom, where they discussed religion and frequently engaged in prayer. He entered their names in a little book and each week there were two or three new names to be added. Generally these meetings were held early in the morning and soon there was an attendance of twenty, something never even heard of in that place before. The meetings grew in interest and in numbers until George's bedroom was not large enough to contain them and it seemed as if the whole staff would be affected from the chiefs down to the youngest apprentices.

One Sunday, when he was crossing Blackfriars Bridge on his way to attend church with another young man, George Williams expressed a wish that he could extend the benefits of his meetings to the assistants in other business firms. He said he felt sure it could be done and it would be a means of blessing to hundreds of young men. The more he thought about it, the more the idea appealed to him and so he called all who were interested to gather in his bedroom on June 6, 1844, and that was the time and place which saw the birth of the Young Men's Christian Association. There were twelve young men present and with one exception they all worked for the same firm. Officers were appointed and a few days later a second meeting was held at which twenty were present. It was decided to rent a room and so one was taken at a rental of sixty cents a week and this was the first outlay for rent. To-day the organization owns property worth millions of dollars. None of the young men had much money to spare, but a collection was taken and enough was raised to pay for the sending out of a letter to the employees of other business houses. The response to this circular was such that a larger hall had to be obtained. The cost of this new room was two dollars a week and it was let to the new society on the strict condition that they would not sing or make too much noise. This room became the headquarters of the Association for the next five years.

There was, of course, considerable opposition to the movement. Some employers pretended to see in it nothing else than a movement for shorter working hours, something they were much opposed to. But the new organization grew steadily. Members of all the different churches were warmly welcomed, and it is interesting to notice that of the first twelve members, three were Episcopalians, three Congregationalists, three Baptists and three Methodists. Mr. Williams was determined that every young man who was willing to observe the rules of the Association should receive a warm

welcome, no matter to what church he belonged.
Each new member was asked to pay twelve cents
and to contribute twelve cents each quarter to the
general fund.

At the end of the first year the Association had
one hundred and sixty members and it was decided
to have a paid secretary. Mr. T. H. Tarlton was
engaged and so became the first secretary of the
Association. Soon the movement began to spread
not only throughout London but to other towns
and cities, and whenever George Williams had a
day's holiday he spent it in visiting some new
branch or in establishing a new one. He kept a
diary and on August 19, 1847, when he was just
twenty-six years of age, he entered in it this
solemn vow: "I do solemnly declare from this
evening to give myself unreservedly to this Association, to live for the prosperity of the Young
Men's Christian Association. I do praise God for
having called me by His grace and so blessed me
temporally . . . I thank Him for the determination to be useful among the young men of the
world."

In 1851 there was a great Exhibition held in
London, one of the largest of its kind ever planned
up to that time. It was designed to bring visitors
from all parts of the world and especially to
stimulate British commerce. It occurred to George

Williams and others that it would be a good opportunity to make known their movement to the people of other countries who would be visiting the Exhibition. Lectures explaining the Association were given and thousands of leaflets were distributed among visitors. These plans proved to be splendidly successful. Before very long there were branches of the Young Men's Christian Association in France, Germany, Australia, India, Canada, and the United States. The movement no longer was confined to England but became a tremendous power in other lands. Not only did it extend to many countries but in every country it did much to break down class prejudice, as young men of all trades and vocations came together in their meetings and learned to understand each other better and respect each other more.

On March 29, 1881, the great Exeter Hall was purchased for the use of the Association. Beginning in George Williams' bedroom, then to a room rented for sixty cents a week, the Association had so grown in thirty-seven years that now one of the finest halls in London was its property. When the great building was formally taken over the famous Earl of Shaftesbury said in his address: "The Young Men's Christian Association is one of the greatest inventions of modern times. It has been the means of providing comfort and encouragement and protection to hundreds of thousands of young men who are to be the future merchants of this country and upon whom this country will rest for its character and even for its safety."

During these years George Williams did not neglect business. He rose steadily step by step until he who arrived in London a poor, unknown youth, glad to work for four dollars a week, became a great merchant. From the beginning he set aside part of his income for the good of others, for kindness and generosity seemed to be in his very blood. As his income increased, his gifts increased. He could be relied upon to support every good cause and what he gave was not something that he would never miss. He lived very simply himself and regularly denied himself in order that he might be able to help needy causes.

The Jubilee of the Young Men's Christian Association was celebrated in London in 1894. From the humble gathering of a few assistants in his bedroom the organization had grown enormously and it was recognized as one of the great forces for good in the world. Delegates to the Jubilee meetings came from every country in Europe and from the United States, Canada, India, Australia, New Zealand, China, Japan, Persia, and South and West Africa. It was the largest religious convention ever held in Great

Britain up till that time. Queen Victoria offered knighthood to George Williams in acknowledgment of the great good he had done to young men throughout the world, and although he did not wish the honour, friends persuaded him that it was the right thing to do, and so he became Sir George Williams. It was a well-deserved honour and the thousands of delegates to the Jubilee Convention were greatly pleased. He was also presented with the freedom of the city of London, another very great distinction.

Sir George Williams lived to pass his eighty-fourth birthday and right up to the day he died the welfare of the Association was his chief interest in life. In November, 1905, he passed peacefully to rest and was buried in St. Paul's Cathedral; when he died there were 7,676 branches of the Young Men's Christian Association in forty-five different countries. The membership was 707,667 and the value of buildings owned amounted to thirty-four million dollars. How many young men the Association had helped during the sixty years since its formation until its founder died, no one can ever tell. Great men and women throughout the entire world were proud to belong to it and both President McKinley and President Roosevelt were among its active members.

The burial in St. Paul's Cathedral on November 14th was one of the most impressive services in the history of that noble building. There is something striking about the pomp of a great military funeral, but there was something much more impressive about the funeral of Sir George Williams. The great busy city seemed to stand still in unspoken tribute as the cortège passed along the streets, which were thronged with reverent onlookers. No doubt the old saying is true that the world loves a fighter, but the fighter it loves most of all is he who fights against the cruel evils that hurt and destroy people; who fights to bring happiness and peace and lasting good into the lives of his fellow men.

XII

WILLIAM H. P. ANDERSON

A Missionary to Lepers

ONE day in 1893 a young man living in Guelph, Ontario, Canada, heard an address in his home church on mission work among lepers. This young man was William Henry Penny Anderson and he was sufficiently interested in what he heard to get the boys in his Sunday-school class to earn what money they could and make a contribution to the Leper Mission.

William Anderson became a chartered accountant, and in 1902 left his home in Guelph to accept a position in Boston, Massachusetts. His interest in the pathetic condition of lepers led him to offer himself as a worker among them. He was accepted and was placed in charge of a large leper colony at Chandkuri, Central India. If William Anderson had been easily discouraged, or had taken up this work without counting the cost, he certainly would have returned to his Canadian home, as the sad plight of the lepers was even worse than he had ever imagined.

This strange disease is one of the oldest in the history of the human race. It is a wasting disease, so loathsome that the poor sufferers have always had a hard time. Very rarely have even their relatives had any pity for them and frequently they have been treated with barbarous cruelty. Sometimes efforts were made to annihilate them and thus try to stamp out the awful plague, and these massacres were attended with almost inhuman cruelty to the lepers. In Great Britain, as in many other countries, lepers were cut off from all social privileges, driven out, and denied the right to mix with their fellows. Often their condition was such that death came to them as a blessed relief.

To-day compassion and loving sympathy have taken the place of hatred and cruelty. The helping hand has been stretched out and the lepers have eagerly reached for it. Here is how William Anderson describes the coming of a leper to the home: "The heat of the sun is relentless. The land lies gasping. Man and beast have sought already the shelter of a friendly hut or the thin shade of a tree. Along a hot, dusty Indian road a poor creature drags himself painfully. No hand offers to help; not even a drink of water can he get. It is well on to midday when he sees in front of him the this name for their home and so that leper colony has been called "Fairyland" ever since.

After Anderson went to India never a day passed without his being brought face to face with the ravages of this awful disease. One day soon after he arrived as he passed along the road eighteen lepers stood holding up their hands which were devoid of fingers. Some of them had feet so mutilated and wasted that they could scarcely stand upright. All of them were in dreadful destitution and with voices made husky by disease, they cried: "Have mercy on us." Anderson never forgot that scene although such painful experiences became a regular occurrence. He solemnly vowed in his heart that he would do all that lay in his power to help these sufferers; a vow he has splendidly fulfilled.

Often it was very difficult to get a poor woman, stricken with leprosy, to give up her yet untainted child. Such mothers, driven out from the society of others, found in the love of sweet babies the one bright spot in the world and so wanted to keep them. Yet the child would surely become infected before long if not taken away. William Anderson, always firm but ever kind, used patient persuasion. At first the mother would be suspicious and fearful, remembering all the cruel treatment she had received. Then gradually these feelings would give place to confidence and gratitude. The mother, after a great struggle and with eyes wet with tears, would bring her child to Mr. Anderson and say: "Take her, Sahib, take her; see, I give her to you."

The work of rescuing untainted children in itself has meant that thousands upon thousands of little folks, who would doubtless have been infected with the loathsome disease and for years would have dragged their weary bodies from place to place until death came as a happy relief, have grown to become perfectly healthy men and women. These rescued people have not been slow to show their deep gratitude and no doubt the heartfelt thanks of such has done much to keep genuine Christians such as William Anderson, and many other devoted workers, at their noble task.

It is a strange thing that in spite of their great distress, most lepers seem eager to help each other and, especially those who have become Christians, are frequently cheerful. Although they live on a few cents a week they make their weekly contributions of rice to church funds. In the leper homes are small earthen vessels and in these are placed such quantities of rice as can be spared. This is taken to church on Sunday and, as the rice basket is passed along the rows, the lepers put in

Two thousand years ago Jesus lived in Palestine and cleansed the lepers. Jesus is no longer here in the flesh, but He lives in men's hearts and through such men as William Anderson He carries on His gracious ministry to these sadly afflicted people.

XIII

JACOB RIIS

Who Wanted Good Homes for All the
People

ONE day a little Danish boy placed a starch box outside his bedroom window, which was on the sunny side of the house, for the birds. A starling made its home in that box and before long there were several blue eggs there. Day by day the boy watched those eggs and when they were hatched and a family of little starlings appeared his joy knew no bounds. Later, when the weather made his old starch box look shabby, he replaced it with a wooden one. This was much larger and a number of sparrows began to crowd out the starlings, whereupon the little fellow wrote this note and fastened it on the box: "This box is for starlings, not for sparrows."

This little lad was Jacob Riis. He was born at Ribe in Denmark on May 3, 1849. When he grew to be a lad of twelve he was still interested in houses, this time not for birds but for people. There was a wretched slum district in Ribe, named

"Rag Hall," and every time he passed, Jacob felt very sorry for the people who lived there. One Christmas he had received a silver mark and was about to spend it on himself but he remembered the poor people in "Rag Hall" so he went there and offered the coin to a man on the express condition that the people should tidy the place up and especially attend to the children. The man took the coin, although he looked stunned at the condition upon which it was given. Young Jacob kept watch on that slum and, sure enough, before long there was considerable whitewashing done and the children looked cleaner.

Jacob's father taught in the town school and was in charge of the Latin class. There were no less than fourteen children in the family and so Jacob went to work at an early age. He was only fifteen when he left for Copenhagen to work for a carpenter. The third day he was in the big city Jacob was wandering along the street, homesick and lonely, when he got into conversation with a very friendly gentleman. This man asked him a few questions and the lad became quite talkative. He told about his home in Ribe, his father, and the school, and indeed about a great many things. It was a great surprise to him later in the day when Jacob found that he had been talking with the King of Denmark.

When he was nineteen he decided to emigrate to the United States, although he had very little money and travelled steerage. He arrived at New York in the early summer of 1870, without knowing anyone in America and with only a few dollars in his pocket. The first few months were full of hardship for the new arrival. He was a stranger in a strange land. He had to take whatever labouring jobs he could get, and he worked harder and had longer hours then than at any time in his life. When each Sunday came and he did not have his work to go to, he wandered aimlessly for miles and miles feeling so lonely that if he had possessed the money doubtless he would have returned to Denmark.

He knew very little English and spoke with a decided foreign accent. Gradually he learned enough of the language to carry on simple conversations and this made things easier for him. The story of the next few years in Jacob's life is a thrilling tale of how a determined lad simply refused to be downhearted even when everything went against him. He had enough hard knocks and disappointments to take the heart out of almost anyone, yet he kept cheerful, with a brave smile upon his lips no matter how heavy he really felt within. He tried his hand at a dozen different jobs. He heard that coal miners were needed some distance away so off he went and worked at that. He hoed cucumbers for three days and at night, weary and aching in every limb, he slept in fields and barns after the day's work was done. For a while he worked in a brick yard at a job for which he was quite unfit, but he did his best and, at least, paid his way. At times he was so hard up he was forced to pawn the few valuables he had brought from home and more than once he slept in a doorway wrapped in a blanket which his mother had given him.

After many months of such experiences he returned to New York with just *one cent* in his pocket. All around the friendless lad there were people apparently happy and prosperous. He trudged along, sick at heart and weary in body. He saw a wagon and climbed into it. He was so tired he fell asleep at once. But he had not noticed that it was a milk wagon and when the driver came in the early morning he quickly dumped Jacob into the gutter. The one thing which occupied his attention now was how to get enough money to cross the sea to his home in Denmark.

One October night, when the rain was falling in torrents, Jacob Riis, soaked through and through, sat on a bank of the river and actually contemplated suicide. He told himself, almost savagely, that nobody cared for him, nobody would miss him, he might as well be dead. Just at that moment he felt a wet shivering body press close beside him, and heard a piteous whine in his ear. It was a little black-and-tan dog, looking even more miserable than he was. Jacob had always been fond of animals and birds even from the days when he placed a starch box outside his bedroom window for the starlings, and there and then he gave up all thoughts of drowning himself. He had something to live for now. This little outcast dog needed him and he decided to take care of it. Later that night the Danish boy got lodging along with scores of others in a miserable police station, but when he complained because a locket he wore had been stolen he was thrown out. The little dog, curled up on the steps, seeing Jacob being ill treated by a bully attacked this man. Much to the boy's dismay the man seized the dog and destroyed it.

After hardships that lasted for several years gradually the tide turned for Jacob Riis and he secured work as a newspaper reporter. When he was appointed to a position on the staff of the *New York Tribune* as police-court reporter at twenty-five dollars a week he thought himself a very wealthy and important man. Now he had a chance to do something for which he had waited many years.

His new duties meant that he had to spend much of his time in a part of the east side of New York known as Mulberry Bend. It was a sordid slum district. His work was chiefly at night and he often walked through the slums for several hours after midnight. What he saw there made him feel that it was not a fit place for people to live and that little children brought up there had not a decent chance to become respectable. Scores of boys and girls in that area became criminals and Jacob Riis used to say he did not wonder at it. There was nothing but poverty and vice all around them and thousands of people were living in filthy tenement houses. When disease broke out the dwellers had no chance. These hovels were a disgrace to the city and a grave menace to both health and morals.

He wrote articles for the newspapers and made speeches in churches and halls whenever he got a chance. He knew that very few people had the faintest idea of the wretched conditions in the slums. Gradually the public conscience was aroused and some people began to encourage him in his fight against these filthy tenements and lodging houses, although others bitterly opposed him. A commission of inquiry was appointed by the city and the first step toward improvement was thus taken.

Typhus fever broke out in the lodging houses

tation as surgeon and physician. At the age of twenty-three he became an army surgeon and when typhoid fever broke out among the troops during the Spanish-American War he was sent there to try to check the havoc it was causing. Dr. Walter Reed became convinced after careful study that yellow fever was caused by the bites of mosquitoes which had become infected by previously biting some person already suffering with the fever. Over and over again with infinite patience Dr. Reed experimented and each experiment helped to confirm him in the belief that he had at last found the cause of this disease which had been such an age-long enemy of the human race.

Two young doctors—James Carroll and Jesse Lazear—went into the fever hospital at Havana and allowed themselves to be bitten by mosquitoes which had previously bitten fever patients. Both these young men were soon taken down with fever and while Dr. Carroll recovered, Dr. Lazear died.

Dr. Reed was now convinced that the terrible yellow fever was caused by mosquitoes and worked harder than ever to gain all the knowledge he could in order to combat it. He appealed for volunteers, making it very clear that those who permitted themselves to be bitten would be running very grave risks. Two young soldiers, John R. Kissenger and John J. Moran, were the first to offer themselves. These young men knew what had happened to Dr. Carroll and Dr. Lazear so what they did was done with open eyes.

Dr. Reed talked very frankly with these two volunteers. He explained the danger involved and what he hoped to accomplish as a result of his experiments. Then he stated the sum of money which the general was prepared to pay to those who offered themselves for experimentation. To Dr. Reed's great surprise both young men declared themselves willing to be experimented on but only upon one condition, and that was, there must be no reward. When Dr. Reed heard this he was deeply moved. "Gentlemen," he said, "I salute you!"

Here is an account of how John Moran was experimented upon: "A sort of mosquito net was prepared for him into which fifteen gnats, all suffering from yellow fever, were admitted. Five minutes afterwards the lad Moran, clad only in a night shirt and fresh from a bath, entered the room, where he lay for a period of thirty minutes. Within two minutes of his entrance he was bitten about the face and hands by the insects that had promptly settled down upon him. Seven infected insects bit him at this visit. At 4.30 p.m. the same day he entered again and remained twenty minutes, during which time five others bit him.

The following day, at 4.30 P.M., he again entered and remained fifteen minutes, during which time three insects bit him, making fifteen in all that had fed upon him during these three visits. On Christmas morning at 11 o'clock this brave lad was stricken with yellow fever and had a sharp attack which he bore without a murmur."

Dr. Walter Reed was now able to demonstrate that the mosquito was responsible for yellow fever and, armed with this knowledge, experts began to study the mosquito. They watched it closely, studied its haunts and habits and began to wage war upon this enemy of mankind.

Once Dr. Reed had demonstrated that the mosquito was responsible for yellow fever its terrible ravages in tropical lands were at once understood. For instance, in Panama the heat at certain seasons is terrific but along with this there are heavy and sustained rainfalls. There were then no proper roads and so the water lay in innumerable pools which soon became stagnant and breeders of disease. The disease-carrying insects bred in millions and went forth, myriads at a time, to do their deadly work. Outwardly Panama was very beautiful, with as rich and varied foliage as could be found anywhere in the world, but thirty years ago it was a veritable forcing bed of disease.

Dr. Reed lived just long enough to see the

battle against the disease-bearing mosquito well begun. He died soon after his important discovery and this knowledge was his last gift to the world —but what a gift it was! The eminent English journalist, Mr. Arthur Mee, wrote: "There is no adventure anywhere more instinct with heroism than the search for the author of yellow fever and its discovery. Even if there had been no gain for freedom in the Spanish-American War, the conquest of yellow fever would have been worth the war a hundred times."

Major-General Leonard Wood, Military Governor of Cuba, said, "I know of no man who has done so much for humanity as Major Reed. His discovery results in the saving of more lives annually than were lost in the Cuban war and saves the commercial interests of the world a greater financial loss in each year than the cost of the entire Cuban war."

Dr. Walter Reed died at the age of fifty-one. He was buried in Arlington Cemetery, Washington, and on the monument at the head of his grave are inscribed these words: "He gave to man control over that dreadful scourge, yellow fever." He was a true hero, always deeply moved at the sight of human suffering. After his great discovery he wrote to his wife: "The prayer that has been mine for twenty years, that I might be permitted in some way or at some time to do something to alleviate human suffering, has been granted." There are thousands who will devoutly thank God that Dr. Walter Reed's prayer was answered.

XV

GEORGE MÜLLER

WHO BUILT ORPHANAGES BY PRAYER

ABOUT the year 1830 there was a remarkable young man preaching in Bristol, England. He spoke with a strong German accent, which made a good deal of what he said difficult to understand, but somehow his kind heart and winning ways caused him to be a much-loved man in the city and throughout the whole countryside.

His name was George Müller and he was born at Kroppenstadt, Prussia, on September 27, 1805. He received a good education in his own country, and when he arrived in England his earnestness and simple straightforward manner made a good impression upon the people.

Great numbers of people at that time in England—as in most other countries—were very poor indeed. A penny loaf of white bread was a luxury. Most children of the labouring class were fed on bran dumplings and even potatoes were seldom seen in many homes. Wherever George Müller looked he saw poverty and suffering. He saw hard-working men and women, grown old before their time, and children with little or no education and generally without sufficient food or clothing.

Müller began to wonder how he could help these people. He himself was a poor man living in a very humble way as pastor of a congregation of earnest but poor people. Yet day and night he was thinking out plans in order to better the lot of destitute children. He prayed earnestly about it and soon a very strange thing happened. A man living hundreds of miles away, whom he had never even seen, sent Müller three hundred dollars to be used for the poor of Bristol.

There were no public schools in those days such as there are now and the ignorance of the young was appalling. Müller began to gather together as many children as he could and taught them to read and sing simple hymns. They were a strange-looking lot of children that came to his schools, with their scanty clothing, and most of them hungry. Many came from filthy alleys where families were crowded together and where clean-liness was unknown. Every day they heard vile language which they themselves were quick to use. Honesty seemed unknown, and nearly every youngster felt justified in stealing whatever he could. There were no bad habits that these un-

fortunate children did not learn. But dirty, un-
kempt, and rough and restless as they might be,
George Müller loved them as though they were
his own children.

Of all the children that came to his schools—
for soon there were five schools with over 450
pupils—Müller was most interested in the orphans. There were thousands of them in the city.
They roamed through the streets and dark alleys,
unowned by parents, uncared for by anybody, so
hungry and ill clothed that they were ever on the
lookout to take food or clothing even when they
had to get it by stealing. They were "street arabs"
and it was no wonder that hundreds of them grew
up to be thieves and burglars. The condition of
children who had parents living was bad enough
but the lot of those who were orphans was ten
times worse and Müller could not get them out
of his mind.

Müller came to the conclusion that he must
establish a home for orphan children, although he
did not have the faintest idea where the money
was to come from. First, the building would have
to be erected, then teachers and matrons secured
and paid, yet he was a poor man living with his
wife on a few dollars a week. He decided that the
only way to realize his ambition was to pray about
it and this he began to do in earnest. He saw much

in the Bible to persuade him that if he had sufficient faith and prayed in the right spirit his prayers would be answered, so he began to pray that God would move the hearts of people to send him money for the orphanage.

Müller decided that he would not follow the usual method of asking people for money either in public or in private. Furthermore he resolved never under any circumstances to go into debt. He would not do any advertising of any kind whatever but trust to his prayers for the desired results. He decided to pray for the sum of five thousand dollars. Two days after he began to pray a twenty-five-cent piece came; that was the first donation. Then a second and a third were sent to him. For two days nothing was received, then there arrived a bale of clothing for the orphans and two dollars and fifty cents. A man sent in a gift of household utensils for the orphanage that he felt sure would be built. Here is a list of this parcel: three dishes, twenty-eight plates, three basins, one jug, four mugs, three salt stands, one grater, four knives, and five forks. Next day, when Müller was at prayer, another parcel arrived. This one contained three dishes, one basin, and a blanket. Then came a gift of two hundred and fifty dollars from a most unlikely source. Next day a man and his wife offered Müller the furniture that was in their

home and also volunteered to work in the orphanage without any salary, feeling sure that their
simple wants would be attended to. Every day gifts
of one kind and another were received and whatever came, no matter how small and insignificant
the gift seemed, George Müller devoutly thanked
God for it. Everything that came, whether money,
clothing, furniture or whatever it was, came un-
asked, for Müller's plan was to lay his needs before
God and trust Him for an answer.

On April 21, 1836, a house was rented at 6 Wil-
son Street, Bristol, and the orphanage was begun.
At first it was restricted to girls, and thirty orphan
girls between the ages of seven and twelve were at
once given a good home. Many of these orphan
girls had younger brothers and sisters and a second
home became absolutely necessary. For nearly
six months Müller prayed for means wherewith to
open a home for orphan infants and for some
devoted person to take care of them. The prayers
were answered; a fine capable woman offered her
services and the second orphanage was opened on
November 28th, in very suitable premises.

Müller began by praying for five thousand dollars, and at the end of eighteen months and ten
days this entire amount had been received. Some
men might have boasted under similar circumstances; not so George Müller. In deep humility

was purchased. Sl[...]
in and the founda[...]
was laid on Augu[...]
gun and proceed[...]
Müller to meet al[...]
thing. The buildin[...]
seventy-five thou[...]
thousand as was[...]
spring of 1849—a[...]
of prayer—the e[...]
tributed and the[...]
opened to receive[...]
folks. On the day[...]
of debt and there v[...]
three thousand do[...]

Some men wou[...]
wonderful achieve[...]
no sooner opened [...]
of homeless child[...]
Müller decided th[...]
date seven hundre[...]
new building woul[...]
five thousand doll[...]
said to his astonis[...]
homeless children[...]

Once again Geo[...]
and his prayers w[...]
age to take care[...]

and gratitude he thanked God that the gifts to begin and carry on the two orphanages had been freely sent, most of them by people whom he had never even seen.

During all these days Müller had to feed and clothe his orphan family, which steadily grew larger. Sometimes he would be at his wit's end for food and clothing but he always made his needs a matter of prayer. Sometimes when the orphans had finished eating there would not be enough food in the house for another meal, yet always the needed money, or food, was sent just in time.

One Saturday Müller was sorely in need of money. There were bills to be met, salaries due, and clothing needed. He realized that he required two hundred and fifty dollars. Over the week-end he laid his case before God in prayer. There was just enough food to give the orphans breakfast, then came the postman with a letter from India containing a gift of exactly two hundred and fifty dollars. Some time later a day came when, with the exception of some potatoes, there was no food in the orphanage within two hours of dinner time. Then came a gift of sixty dollars, just in time to enable Müller to buy provisions for the next meal. One morning after the children had been fed there was just five cents left. In the two orphanages every loaf of bread had been cut and

the outlook
noon a gift c
and the emer
    Meanwhile
too small for
ler resolved
hundred chil
grow vegetab
This meant h
dollars and h
as he had rai
out asking an
going into de
he had yet a
pectations we
for thirty-six
thousand dol
ever receive
offered to pr
age free of ch
Müller and in
home came in
but all receiv
God. Many o
whom Müller
people living
of earnest pr
sand dollars

opened on November 12, 1857, and another home to accommodate three hundred more was ready on March 12, 1862. By this time he had a family of more than a thousand homeless waifs and strays to whom he was all that a kind father could be. The children were clothed, fed and given such education as was possible, with the result that thousands of boys and girls were well taken care of who otherwise would have been utterly neglected and in many cases would have become criminals.

He lived to open a fourth orphanage on November 5, 1868, and a fifth one on January 6, 1870, and was thus able to care for considerably more than two thousand orphans. The five orphanages he had built and maintained by prayer caused people everywhere to marvel at Müller's simple but strong faith. When he was visiting Europe the Queen of Württemberg sent for him and asked particulars about his orphanages. The fact that he had raised vast sums of money without asking people for it made men realize that there was something which could not be explained in the ordinary way.

George Müller died on March 10, 1898, at the advanced age of ninety-three. Four days later one thousand of the elder boys and girls from the orphanage gathered around his coffin for a simple service. As his remains were borne through the streets of Bristol there were extraordinary demonstrations of sorrow, showing the very high regard in which this man of prayer had been held. Over the great cathedral a flag flew at half mast; street cars were halted and for a time practically all traffic in the city ceased. When thousands of orphan children, to whom he had been as a father, walked in the procession, onlookers devoutly thanked God that such a man had lived in their midst.

At the time of his death over ten thousand orphan children had been taken care of in the Müller homes and the money sent to him for the building and maintenance of these orphanages alone totalled five million dollars. This was not the whole of his life work but it is the achievement by which he will be best remembered. Although he had raised millions for others, when George Müller died he left very little more than the clothes he was wearing and a few articles of furniture.

THE END